Wha

"Linda shares an amazing and deeply personal story. Who could have imagined that God could use a tragic accident in the Canadian north in the mid-1900s to cause an increasing ripple effect of blessing today? And we'll never know the end of Linda's story until we get to heaven and learn how her story affected yours, and mine."

Rick Bergen, President, Missão Marabá, Brazil

"This book is an invitation. We are taken on a journey across the Canadian Prairies to pinpoint a time when a young woman on a tractor meets her defining moment. This is a story of her journey of love, self-forgiveness, and eventually freedom. Linda A. Olson has once again brought healing through pain, as she teaches me - through her story."

Kathleen D. Mailer, International Business Evangelist, #1 Best Selling Author, including "Walking In The Wake of the Holy Spirit, Living An Ordinary Life,With an Extraordinary God", Founder/Facilitator of "A Book Is Never A Book Boot Camp", Editor-In-Chief of Today'sBusinesswoman Magazine.

Once I began reading Linda's riveting story, I could not put it down. If you have ever experienced loss of any kind or guilt, you owe it to yourself to read this book. You will be encouraged, uplifted, and you will know that a future filled with hope is truly possible.

Valeria Vick, www.BookitVal.com

"Beautifully and compellingly written, God's story of triumph over tragedy in Linda's life will illuminate your path, no matter how dark and grim.

If you believe you cannot forgive yourself in the face of seemingly insurmountable pain, you must read this book. In its pages, lies the hope and healing you deserve."

Leslie J. Smith, B.A., LL.B. Lawyer, Mediator, Deputy Judge, Author, Speaker www.legaleasecanada.com

I love Linda Olson's writing style in her book, "His Ways Are Higher," It is full and engaging, keeping you reading and evoking powerful emotions. You will find the story gripping and taking you on a roller coaster of anger and sadness. I highly recommend this book as it will impact and change you to be even better than you are now.

Glen Klassen, Author of "Unlimited - Anything is Possible" www.gleneklassen.com

Fasten your seat belts and hold on tight! This will be one of those books that you will not be able to put down! Linda will take you on a step by step account into her childhood and allow you to experience with her (as if you were back in time) into the moments of her life which give vivid accounts of a traumatic time that would later serve to bring healing for those desperately needing to see the light at the end of the tunnel. It is her testimony of found hope and healing that will encourage anyone going through their own valley of the shadow of death.

Emma Vega, UMC Spanglish Co-Director A ministry targeting 1st, 2nd, 3rd generation Hispanic/Latino Young People The United Methodist Church, California-Pacific Conference FB: UMC Spanglish / IG: umc_spanglish / #SpanglishNOW

Linda writes a compelling story of heartbreak and the long journey to self-forgiveness. She explores some hard questions and shares the gentle answers that God gave her in her time of need. Her story is one of grief, hurt and ultimately triumph as she allowed God to minister His grace, forgiveness and love to her hurting places. Join her as she encourages you on a journey of self-forgiveness.

Barb Tatlock, Author of "Living Life After Anti-depressants-Emerging From the Shadows of the Vault"

"Linda's life story is compelling. She's a leader and an inspiration to many men and women challenging our walk and purpose. Her hearts desire is to see each individual grow and be the best 'he or she' they can be! She allows her suffering and pain to create blessings that bring us a life-giving message of hope that pierced my heart in her new book, His Ways are Higher.

Connie Thieman, Pastor of Kid's Ministry

"Linda transparently chronicles the rippling effect of personal, brutal tragedy at a young age, sharing deeply the heartbreaking agony of feeling alone in the midst of horrendous guilt and grief. His Ways are Higher describes her journey in detail, giving a message of hope and healing to all of us who face life's unbearable hurts. Through her story, Linda assures us that emotional, relational, and spiritual healing really can be ours."

C. J. Chatham, editor and collaborative writer

This was a beautiful, poignant story that touched me deeply. As I read Linda's personal journey of an experience too painful for words, Linda captured my heart immediately with her rich story telling about the simple, but hard life of farming and the painful accident that changed her life forever more. In the tenderness in which she describes looking into her baby brother's eyes, as he lay dying in her arms, you can feel the overwhelming sense of loss. A story of life with the fullness of the good and bad, and sorrow and joy, with a unique redemptive quality that makes it hard to put down as you anticipate the healing and hope that is sure to come.

Carol L. Doyel, Founder, Editor-in-Chief Living Better 50

"You can't give what you don't have. To truly be able to walk in love and forgiveness towards others, we must be able to forgive and love ourselves first. Through Linda's heartfelt story that takes you from personal tragedy, to forgiveness, to healing...she so richly demonstrates God's incredible gift of grace and mercy, and His overwhelming ability to inevitability work all things together for our good. This is certainly a must read for anyone who desires healing and hope in their lives!"

Bill Pavelich, CEO and Founder, PerspectivEdge

"Being a big city girl, I loved the country girl perspective in Linda's book about her life, challenges, and God's love. Her writing style draws you in and you may find it hard to put down this true-life story of hope, healing, and life-after a crushing loss."

Marnie Swedberg, International Leadership Mentor, www.Marnie.com

"His Ways Are Higher," is a must read for everyone. I have known Linda Olson for several years and to see *the transformation in overcoming the impossible is an inspiration to all. Linda Olson is a godly woman and brings hope for all with this story. I highly recommend this book.*

Barbara Marshall, CEO BarbTV & The Barb Marshall Show (707) 489-3722, Barb@barbTV.org, www.barbtv.org

Everyone has a story. Linda's story will grip your heart. It portrays a woman of prayer, faith, and amazing courage. This book is a page turner and a reminder that even when life makes no sense, God is in still in control. We serve a God of miracles and Linda is one of them.

Sharon Hill, Founder,OnCall Prayer™ Ministries OnCallPrayer.org, Author of the OnCall Prayer Journal & The Power of Three - How a Protective Shield of Intentional Prayer Can Transform Your Life

"Leadership is a willingness to share our stories and our struggles with others in hopes of guiding them in their own lives. By opening her heart and sharing her story, Linda Olson unpackages her personal journey to forgiveness and leads us down a path to do the same. I hope that you are as challenged by her as I have been!"

Christie Love, Founder and Executive Director of LeadHer, www.leadher.org

Linda shares a poignant personal story. She takes the reader through a very difficult experience. She then compels the reader to join her on her journey to wholeness.

Dr. Katherine Warnock, R 'N R Counseling (Restructuring 'N Restoring), www.rnrcounseling.com, Email:doctormom@telus.net

On any ordinary day, at any moment something unexpected can happen that will affect the rest of your life. Whether we feel it or not God is there with us, but how we respond is our choice. Let Linda's spiritual journey of heartache and discovery help speed you over the unavoidable roadbumps along your way. Learning from other's experience is wisdom and it's much easier!

Rev. Gwen Ehrenborg, Living Witnesses Ministries, Founder , Supporting Women In Ministry International, President www.swiminternational.org/ United Methodist Minister; General Evangelist

Linda's powerful story will grip your whole being as you read the passages that reveal her horrific heartbreak. Her journey of self-forgiveness, courage and inspiration is her gift to us as she shares how she takes hold of God's love, His grace and His mercy. This is real life, real pain and heartbreak that has been graciously molded into true hope and victory as Linda has looked to her Heavenly Father for answers to her brokenness. Thank you Linda, for sharing your heart with us!

Margie McIntyre,, Author of "Mind Matters - Change Your Mind, Change Your Life!"
www.mindmattersseries.com

"Comfort! Hope! Understanding! Let your heart be encouraged in every way as you turn these pages. Linda Olson has captured the wisdom that will carry you through your darkest moment. Let transforming light shine into your life as you read this story of triumph in the face of tragedy."

Glenna Salsbury, Professional Speaker, Author of The Art of the Fresh Start

Through this powerful book, Linda shares her story of facing one of the toughest heartaches and asks the question that was buried so deep in her heart, "Why was I the one on the tractor that took little Billy's life?" Miraculously, God answered that question and brought complete healing 45 years later. It is a story of God's grace, love and forgiveness.

Joanne Wallace-Lovelace, Author, Speaker and Optimal Health Living Coach and Mentor.
Email: joannewallacelovelace@gmail.com

*In **His Ways Are Higher**, Linda Olson shares a gripping, descriptive recollection of a personal trauma that occurred in her life, as a 14-year old girl. This was a trial*

by fire that could only be lessened by her faith, the passage of time and a lengthy, painful grieving. It remains part of who she is and the creation of her recent book **"His Ways are Higher:"** is a testament to this event.

Woven within the pages of this book, she examines how her current religious beliefs differed from those she grew up with and how she came to deeply believe the scripture verses of Isaiah 55:8,9 on forgiveness, specifically self-forgiveness.

This book is inspirational, historical, insightful, has a sense of time and place and offers value to any reader.

Brian Lukyn, Author of The Un-Retirement Guide™
brianlukyn.com

Though I've never lived through a tragedy like Linda experienced, I have through the years struggled with deep depression, and I am grateful to have this book on my shelf for those days that seem more than I can bear. Linda's story is a beautiful confirmation of God's ability to turn trauma into triumph. If you've ever felt pain so deep that you did not believe you could — or even wanted — to survive, this book was written for you, or for someone for whom you care deeply who desperately needs hope.

Barbara Hemphill, Author, Less Clutter More Life

Linda's story of strength, courage and faith will serve as an encouragement to many. It is a message of hope and forgiveness for anyone facing a dark hour. Breakthrough is on its way. A must read for anyone who is hurting.

Lorraine Jacyszyn, Author of Diapers, Desperation & Diplomas: Parenting with Intent

Linda's life journey from unimaginable pain to healing is a powerful story of a young girl becoming a caring God loving woman. God has directed her life in areas of learning to trust him again. May the lessons Linda experienced give you hope in finding peace from your deep hurts.

Bev Burton, Author of "Create Your Calm Waters and Breakthrough Coach

Thank you Linda for sharing your heart with us in this powerful book! Faith in the tragedies and trusting God no matter what. A story of hope.

Diane Cunningham, M.Ed., Founder and President National Association of Christian Women Entrepreneurs, www.nacwe.org, Author of 6 books including the Rock Bottom is a Beautiful Place Amazon best selling book series.

This inspirational book by Linda spells out hope beyond your worst nightmare. This book will challenge you to dust off the debris of disillusionment and perplexity indiscriminately forced on you by life and to keep walking, looking up to God for strength.

Godlove Ngufor, Author of Empowering Potential: Re-birthing the African Entrepreneurial spirit.

His Ways are Higher is a powerful story of hope and forgiveness. The author skillfully takes us on her journey of triumph, amidst a terrible tragedy. In varying degrees, we have all faced times in our life that are dark and sad and lonely. Let your heart soar as you triumph alongside Linda for your soul is sure to be touched as you read this story.

Suzanne D Jubb, Speaker, Trainer and Author of The Golden Goose, One Important Step to Financial Freedom

Linda Olson bares her soul in this very personal story. Reaching for a life of fruitfulness, Linda demonstrates how to follow God's leading even when life doesn't make sense and the questions are many. His Ways Are Higher is a beautiful story of faith and forgiveness that is sure to resonate with and encourage the hearts of many.

Kate Janzen, Author of Moving Forward After Betrayal, www.movingforwardafterbetrayal.com, Email: kate.janzen2015@gmail.com

Linda Olson has done it again. Her book is a true gift to the Kingdom of God. The principles and practices that Linda develops in His Ways Are Higher are not just theory. They come from her own life experience as a woman of God and professional Christian Counselor. I am confident this book too will transform the lives of many.

Ken Hart, Founding Pastor, Lead Pastor, The Highlands Christian Fellowship

His Ways Are Higher

One Woman's Journey of
Self-Forgiveness Against Unbeatable Odds

by

Linda A. Olson

with

C. J. Chatham

Published by Made for More Enterprises, Inc.

Made for More Enterprises offers the purchase of this book in bulk for any form of education, business, fund-raising or sales promotion use.

For more information please e-mail our Special Marketing division at: linda@madeforsomethingmore.com

Unless otherwise noted, scripture quoted in this book is from the NKJV which is the New Kings James Version.

Library of
Olson, Linda A. His Ways Are Higher, One Woman's Journey of Self-Forgiveness Against Unbeatable Odds.

This Book Is Dedicated To

To the Lord Jesus Christ who miraculously took me from my darkest moment to living life and living it more abundantly. When I didn't know if it was possible to go on, He gave me the strength and courage to step forward. When I longed for answers He gave me a promise in Isaiah 58:8,9. When I didn't expect to receive an answer to my deepest question, "Why was I on the tractor that took Billy's life that day?", He answered it in a very specific way, 44 years later. My heart is deeply grateful for His presence, His promise and His faithfulness.

Acknowledgements

to those who have lovingly, patiently and graciously stood by me. It's because of your influence and impact in my life, I am who I am today.

A great big thank you to:

My parents who have re-united with their son in eternity. Through all their pain they never blamed me for the loss of their beloved son.

My brother and sisters who always reached out a loving hand when their hearts were crushed as well.

My **extended family, friends and relatives** who came alongside me and helped carry me through my darkest hours, weeks and years.

Lila (Klassen) Martens, cousin and friend, who came alongside me in High School to help fill those lonely hours and encouraged me to join her at Bible College.

Mentors such as **H. Norman Wright** who shared my pain through graduate school, **Yvonne Gold**, counselor, who walked me through my darkest hour and led me to letting go of my guilt to accept the gift of self-forgiveness, **Dr. Bill Emard**, chiropractor, who often mentored me. It was through him that God brought complete healing 45 years later.

Prayer partners; particularly **Margaret Buhler (Aunt), Teri White (friend)** and **Carl Dyck (cousin)** in my later years as they faithfully prayed for me and my family as well as throughout the writing of this book.

Guy Morrell-Stinson, photographer, who willingly shared his time and expertise.

Cindy Chatham, collaborative writer, who lovingly shared her gifts with me as we journeyed together for four years through the writing of this book.

Kathleen Mailer, who encouraged me, offered wisdom and insights and prayed for me through the writing and marketing process.

Our daughters, **Melinda & Karine**, who were there for me in ways they don't even know. When the pain surfaced and I didn't know what to do… they reached out a loving hand.

My faithful and committed husband, **Rick Olson**, who supported me through many tears, was always ready to pray with me and reach out a loving heart.

"Thank you to all of you—you know who you are— who have prayed with me and for me over the years." I am asking God to bless each one of you, as well as each one who reads this book, in a way that I never can.

Introduction

What does a young person do when she is derailed from her expectations of the future?

What happens when life one moment is benevolent and sweet and the next moment darker than even the most unimaginable nightmare?

*****

Dear Reader,

Growing up as an ordinary farm girl struggling to find my identity, I often wondered how courageous I really was. A family tragedy led me to ask the same questions that have been asked for generations: *What do you do when you can barely hang on*? *How can a loving God let this happen*? *What do you do when God is silent*? I found that some days I could barely put one foot in front of the other because of grief and sorrow.

But slowly—some days ever so slowly—I began to put one foot in front of the other with more confidence, with a greater understanding of life. Instead of simply wishing my pain would go away, I discovered I could choose to walk *through* my grief-based pain with forgiveness and, more specifically, self-forgiveness.

My walk of horrific pain and guilt ultimately led me to find strength, faith, and courage in God alone. I had many questions, and eventually, only one answer. The scripture verses found in Isaiah became my lifeline:

> *For My thoughts are not your thoughts, Nor are your ways My ways, says the LORD.*

> *For as the heavens are higher than the earth, So are My ways higher than your ways, And My thoughts than your thoughts.*

> Isaiah 55:8,9 (NKJV)

I came to believe with all my heart that *His Ways Are Higher,* and I pray my story may help you find a message of hope and forgiveness in your own dark hour.

Sincerely,
Linda

Table Of Contents

Prologue

Mom, standing in the entryway of our 1959 farmhouse, her breakfast apron speckled with bread crumbs from making our sandwiches, waved as we boarded the bus. "Don't forget! As soon as you come home from school, change your clothes and help with the potatoes." Her shouts barely reached our ears before the bus door unfolded to close out the crisp morning chill. Violet, Leonard, Vera, and I hurriedly settled onto the green vinyl bench seats just moments before the gas engine lurched us forward.

Fall harvest was in full swing. Our family of seven knew firsthand about "if you don't work, you don't eat" and we didn't complain. Cracking open a steaming baked potato in the dead of winter was reward enough for our labors. Nodding my head briefly to Mom through the bus window, I settled into my own world for the hour-long ride.

I thought of the school I had attended last year. The imitation red-brick building had sheltered my father while he mastered his sums and learned the alphabet. For eight years, in the same one-room

1

Linda A. Olson

schoolhouse, I had recited poetry and drawn maps of foreign countries, happily studying with thirty other children who lived in our small Canadian community. The hardwood desks, arranged by grade, were the academic nests of friends and family. Our distant neighbor Herb, my step-uncle Walter, and I all had wrapped our growing adolescent frames around the chairs in the coveted well-lit area next to the windows of the schoolroom, the place reserved for eighth-graders.

Now the country schools had consolidated, and students rode a bus into town to gain the benefits of more formal education. Although I could hardly complain about getting a ride—trudging through fifteen inches of snow for three-quarters of a mile in forty-degree-below-zero weather was not my idea of fun—getting up before dawn to ride the bus an hour every morning meant an hour's ride every night only to arrive home at twilight. The Bergen children, as we were known, were the first to board the bus and the last to leave.

Now those days were behind me, and I was growing up—much faster than I wanted, to be sure. Meager attempts at finding my identity blurred among seventy-five freshmen classmates. Our high school student body topped out at two hundred fifty pupils—hardly the cozy, intimate circle of friends that I had hoped would welcome a local farm girl.

His Ways Are Higher

After the day's lessons and the long ride home, I hopped down the steps of the bus and lugged my book bag to my bedroom. I changed clothes—work in the garden required well-worn denim jeans and a hand-me-down loose, long-sleeved cotton shirt—and stopped in the kitchen to quickly make a peanut butter-and-jelly sandwich. Tossing the dirty knife into the dishpan, I hurried to the garden to join the others.

Over one hundred sixty acres surrounded our three-bedroom farmhouse. We must have looked like a bullseye from the air, with our property being surrounded by towering trees, cultivated fields, and a country road. Our vegetable garden lay northwest of the front of the house, a bit of an unusual location but one that caught the necessary six hours of afternoon sunlight. Taking a bite of my sandwich, I pushed open the front screen door with my foot and saw that Mom had recruited some extra help for the day's task. Grandma, on crutches but eager to help, and Grandpa Warkentin along with Aunt Laurie nodded their greetings. Three-year-old Karen, Aunt Laurie's older daughter, played with my little brother. Billy was two years old and melted everyone's heart with his bib overalls, bare feet, and winsome smile. He tagged along everywhere, always wanting to be part of the action. Today that action would include burrowing beneath the wilted potato leaves in our Manitoban soil to dig out the Red Russet

Linda A. Olson

and Golden Yukon potatoes which would be stored in the basement for the winter.

Mom looked out across the front field, her hand shielding her eyes from the late afternoon sun. She spoke quietly, within earshot of Grandpa. "Last year we took so many trips with the pails; today we'll use the front-loader to bring the potatoes right up to the front step, as close as we can get to the house."

Grandpa nodded, and Mom glanced my way. She must have seen the question in my eyes. My ears had perked up at the overheard suggestion and I was mutely anticipating her next words. Remembering how my arms had ached last year after hauling two five-gallon pails full of potatoes for hours, I would dearly love to avoid the myriad trips from the garden to the basement in the late-September heat.

"Would you like to drive, Linda?"

I broke into a smile. At only fourteen, I was already an old hand at driving the Cockshutt 35 tractor. Taking a turn driving large farm equipment was a common responsibility for most teenagers in the area, bridging the gap between childhood chores and essential farming tasks on the family homestead.

Mom continued her instructions. "We'll pile the potatoes in the front-end loader. When it's full, Linda, drive it to the front of the house. Then we'll unload it with the pails and carry the potatoes to the basement."

She didn't need to repeat her words. I nodded my obedience and quickly ran to climb the thirty-four-inch tire, boosting myself into the red metal seat. I could already taste the dust flying in the autumn air, envisioning the tractor bouncing its way along the well-worn path to the house.

*****

I parked the tractor near the garden where I joined Grandpa, Mom, Violet, and Vera. We emptied pail after pail of potatoes into the bucket of the front-end loader until it could hold no more without spilling. Now it was time to head back to the house. Hopping once again into the metal seat, I positioned myself behind the wheel and turned the key. I peered over the top of the faded yellow tractor and, carefully shifting into reverse, backed the vehicle away from the garden, turning the steering wheel to change directions. Next I shifted into drive and steered the 5,000 pound tractor toward the doorway of our pink stucco farmhouse. Billy and Karen played on the front step, watching my approach.

I neared the house and released the hand throttle, one foot on the clutch and the other on the brake. *This was so much easier than toting heavy pails*, I thought. *We'll be finished in no time.* I pressed the brake, anticipating the deceleration of the Cockshutt.

It didn't happen.

The tractor didn't slow, didn't obey my command to slow its pace.

I gripped the steering wheel for leverage and pressed harder on the brake. The huge machine refused to slow. Alarmed, I realized the house was rushing up too quickly. I gathered all my strength, slid off the seat to a standing position and, with all my weight, jammed my foot on the brake, pumping up and down, up and down, demanding that the wheels stop their turning.

No response.

Bewildered and confused, I sensed the betrayal of the machine beneath me, rejecting my efforts to bring it under control. Quickly it was swallowing the distance to the house. I locked eyes with Mom, silently pleading for split-second direction; all I saw was my own panic reflected in her eyes. I screamed the only explanation I knew.

"I can't stop the tractor!"

I kept jumping on the brake. The tractor aimed for the house as if it was an arrow headed for its mark. I stomped on the brake, the clutch, then the brake again. Nothing. I turned my head slightly to catch any sound of Mom telling me what to do, but all I could hear was the engine growling its refusal to halt.

I could see that Mom was screaming now, but I couldn't make out her words. I put all my weight on the steering wheel and lifted myself up slightly and came down hard on the brake with all the force I could muster. *Oh, God, what do I do? The house is close—too close. I can't stop the tractor, Mom! I can't stop…!*

Mom shrieked as the front-end loader slammed into the stucco wall of the house and white wooden doorframe. The impact threw me forward into the steering wheel. I straightened my body and heard the horrific sounds of splitting wood as the doorframe dismantled. But, the kids! *Where were the kids? Where was Billy?*

The tractor had slammed into the house exactly where Karen and Billy stood. Billy, attempting to escape the huge machine that was barreling toward him, had taken one step in front of the stucco house, almost as if to mark his destiny.

The machine, its angry rumble still spitting fury, had halted its impulsive rampage just inside the double door. Through the swirling furry I saw Karen's colorful floral blouse wedged between the splintered panels. Quiet whimpering told me she was alive— *thank God!*—and I strained to hear Billy's little-boy sobs. But I could hear only Mom screaming above the noise of the engine. And this time I could make out her words.

"My son is dying! My son is dying!"

My eyes swept the scene wildly, looking for the baby brother who giggled and chased fireflies. My heart cried the words my lips could not form.

Where was Billy?

Mom, in three steps, sprang toward me and vaulted up the Cockshott. Landing beside me, she jerked the gear shift into reverse, and forced the family-friend-turned-enemy to back away from its prey. Then she yanked the key and killed the engine of the mad beast. We leapt off its back simultaneously and, seeing what we didn't want to see, ran to the crumpled overall-clad form on the concrete step.

Billy.

Whitkoph

Chapter One

My brain shifted into auto-pilot. Get Billy. *Get Billy!*

I ran to the limp figure that only moments before had been playing with a bug on the porch with Karen. Grandpa frantically threw the broken boards of the front doors behind them as Aunt Laurie grabbed little Karen. Out of the corner of my eye I saw Mom hurdle the rubble to what had been the entry to the house. A moment later she leapt over the shattered doorframe—now empty of sheltering Karen—and bolted to the silver-grey Ford sedan parked in the garage, car keys in hand.

Scooping up Billy, I wrapped one arm under, one arm over the too-still shoulders, the same way I had held him as a newborn. His semi-conscious form molded easily into my body as I spun around with him to race after Mom to the car. Vera was close behind.

I noticed that Billy's face bore the smudge marks of a little-boy swipe at a runny nose. Instinctively I knew who would go and who would stay. Violet would hold down the fort, preparing supper while delegating

Linda A. Olson

evening chores to Leonard when he returned from the field. Busy hands had always been Violet's way of helping in a crisis. Aunt Laurie would drive Grandma, Grandpa, and Karen to the hospital while stopping for a moment to pick up Uncle George.

*****

And Billy. *Billy!*

Even as I cradled his semi-conscious form in one arm and grabbed the door handle of the Ford with the other, I could not comprehend his injuries. Accidents were common in farming communities, and I knew that in the midst of an emergency, hands moved while hearts prayed. But now my head also pounded with slicing questions. *Why wouldn't the tractor stop? Did I do something wrong? Why didn't I turn the wheel harder? Why did this happen? Billy isn't really hurt badly, is he? Why didn't that tractor stop?*

*****

Although my name was Linda, my uncles often called me "Whitkoph", the German word for "whitehead" because my hair was platinum blonde. I was shy and inhibited, not at all like my oldest sister Violet. At eighteen, she was Mom's right hand helper, often shepherding the younger children through the days' chores and lessons. I was second-born and my job was to pick up the slack and do what I was told, which was fine with me. Sometimes, however, I asserted myself without backing down, especially when it came to sleep.

"Violet, *please* stay on your side tonight." I pulled the quilts over my shoulders as I turned over. The double-bed in the front bedroom provided ample room for two teenage girls, and we usually didn't squabble over everyday matters. Yet Violet's deep slumber often triggered a sprawling advance to my side of the bed, nudging me ever closer to the edge where I would lie, tense and uncomfortable, in a half-awakened stupor. Mom always called to us before dawn, so the hours in bed always seemed too short. The cows did not appreciate Mom being late for the milking, and tardiness in chores only meant tardiness for breakfast, so we dared not drift back to sleep once we heard Mom's voice.

Now irritated at the memory of not getting adequate rest the night before, I drew an imaginary line on the sheets and spoke again to my older sister. "There. No crossing. Hear?" I plumped my feather pillow, smiled my good-night to Vi to let her know I was half-kidding, and nestled under the three hand-stitched quilts Mom had carefully crafted.

My subdued personality fed on quiet discovery and new opportunities, and farm life coupled with school lessons supplied an ample supply of both. I was most comfortable when I was around "babies an' old folk", as my folks would say. True enough, I loved people. Really. Seemed to me that a stranger was only a friend I hadn't met. Everyday spats didn't bother me much, and being quick to forgive and quick to ask forgiveness were mainstays in my relationships. I saw life as only good. Full of hard work, to be sure, but good.

*****

I crawled into the back seat of the Ford. Almost before I could shut the door, Mom spun the car out of the dirt driveway toward the nearby quarter of our land where Dad was plowing the field. She leaned her head out the open window.

"Accident!" she screamed.

Dad knew by Mom's face that something terrible had happened, and he knew not to question the declaration. As Dad yanked open the driver's side door to jump behind the wheel, Mom dove over to the passenger seat. Dust and gravel flew everywhere as we barreled down the road at ninety miles an hour to Winnipegosis General Hospital, nine miles away.

Generational Glimpses

Chapter Two

Dad stared forward, his gaze never wavering from the narrow gravel road. His calloused hands gripped the ebony steering wheel as they always did—fingers on top, thumbs below. Now I could see those thumbs and fingers moving back and forth around the circle, clenching into fists. His eyes darted from road to rearview mirror to side mirror to the road again. Mom, turning on the blue vinyl seat to see Billy better, spoke quietly to Dad, her quavering voice summarizing what had happened. Dad's response was clipped.

"Nothing wrong with those brakes."

It was a sentence that would haunt me for years. Although Dad would never blame me directly for the accident, his words underscored my own frantic search for the reason that caused the little boy who lay in my arms to become weaker as the color drained from his rosy little cheeks.

*****

Mom always deferred to Dad, partly because the head of the home always had the last word in a German family and partly because Mom knew it was useless to argue with a stubborn man. Both Mom and Dad were children of immigrants, Mom's parents having come to Canada in 1925 in search of employment after the start of World War I. They farmed in Southern Manitoba for a few years then moved to Winnipegosis, about 300 miles north, the first Mennonites to settle in the area. Eventually more families in the faith joined them and, in early 1931, a Mennonite church was officially established. Taking turns having worship services in their homes, fathers shared the privilege of reading a chapter from the *PredigchtBuch* (the Sermon Book) or leading the discussion of a Bible chapter.

Mennonite folk work hard, often relying on brute strength to build homes from trees felled on the land and hauled to the local sawmill. Back then, one-quarter acre of land could be purchased for as little as one hundred dollars. The largest cash expense my grandparents had was for the purchase of nails. Grandma and Grandpa bought some land, then added another quarter-acre of sagebrush, rock, and pasture-land for the Holsteins they planned to raise for beef. Eventually they managed to cultivate the soil by "scrubbing", a common term used to describe the chopping of bushes by hand. A hired man with a John Deere tractor and a sturdy break plough churned out the roots. The family would shake out the remains by hand for days before the land was disked repeatedly with horses. Stones, picked out one by one to insure completely cultivated soil, formed a makeshift wall around the perimeter of the garden. Although survival forced the close-knit Mennonite community to work hard, the unwritten rule of neighborliness declared that help was available whenever it was needed.

My mother and father met at the only Mennonite church in the area, getting to know each other through youth activities. Horse-and-buggy rides to and from church provided un-chaperoned occasions for conversation. They married in 1948 after Dad purchased land.

The house on the property, however, was uninhabitable so the young newlyweds spent their first year of wedded life at the home of my mother's parents.

Five children came along during the next eighteen years on that rocky Canadian soil—three daughters and two sons. Late one night, when I was about seven years old, I overheard my parents talking about moving to Ontario, the next province over, to work with cousins who owned a construction firm. Our current home, old and rickety, could no longer withstand the long, harsh Manitoban winters, and moving would be one answer to the housing dilemma. The other option was to remain where we were and to borrow money to build a house, hoping hard work and perseverance would provide enough money to pay off the debt. I could hear anxiety in their voices as they discussed their concerns about caring for our large family. Eventually they decided to stay, determining to raise us where we were. With hard work and perseverance, they would make a go of it.

Mennonites are a quiet people—almost too quiet. My family never expressed extreme emotion, and we never, ever talked about anger or disappointment or sorrow. Communication was often brash and lacked sensitivity or compassion. Children, valued mainly for their strength and hard work, contributed to the family good without resentment. Our parents, not overtly affectionate with us or with each other, could only be coaxed into a quick, embarrassed peck between them when they heard family and friends clang spoons against water-glasses at a rare anniversary celebration. Vacations were limited to a day at the National park or seeing relatives. Our days focused mainly on work.

A strong belief in God threaded through our family, yet it was a rigid faith, relying more on the "thou shalt's" and the "thou shalt not's" expressed in the Scriptures than the fundamentals of knowing God personally. Watching movies downtown was avoided because "you never know who may see you walking into the theatre". Years later, the opinion of the local Saturday afternoon entertainment would be relaxed somewhat.

Every morning before breakfast Mom led us in family devotions, usually reading a short page from *The Daily Bread*, and then saying a brief prayer. Occasionally we bowed our heads and uttered a memorized grace, sometimes in German. Mom seemed to have a more one-on-one relationship with the Lord than Dad did, so she insisted we attend Sunday school and church every week. Later in life, Dad came just for the church service. One day I asked Mom if Dad was a Christian and she said he was, yet it would be many years before he would speak aloud about God and heaven and take a genuine interest in spiritual matters. Eventually, after Mom passed away, he would adopt Mom's custom of reading *The Daily Bread* each morning, and on Sundays he would faithfully pick up several people to take to church with him.

Sunday services in our local church, conducted by well-meaning but untrained men and women, lacked evidence of any sincere joy associated with salvation. Our families dutifully sang all the verses to several hymns, soberly listened to the brief message that resembled a short devotional more than a sermon, and we children, at least, counted the minutes until the final prayer signaled the coming concluding announcements. In all of our spiritual doings, the Holy Spirit was never mentioned.

At home, our relationships carried a sober undertone as well. Disagreements between my parents often ended with Dad raising his voice and Mom withdrawing from the confrontation, suppressing angry tears and sadness. Only a few times did I see her attempt to assert her own opinion more than once in an attempt to stand up to his commanding authority.

Dad, with his strong and bold exterior, really had a tender heart, yet he had great difficulty letting his growing family see it. Mom, on the other hand, was sweet and loving and generous to a fault, but she often carried a heavy heart. Dad answered questions with a blunt "Yes" or "No" and seldom conversed about anything personal. He did not respect Mom's ideas, often disregarding them verbally in front of us children.

Still, through the years, Mom found ways to fill her emotional hunger for companionship. Talks with her sisters helped, their fingers flying quickly with crochet thread or knitting yarn, but everyone avoided discussing personal troubles. Conversing with us children also sometimes seemed to ease

His Ways Are Higher

Mom's loneliness created by an emotionally distant husband. Prayer was vital to her survival. She poured her soul into her diary, writing sometimes with only a few words about the tragedies in life. Later she included photographs in her personal history.

*****

The speedometer on the 1962 Ford approached ninety. Silence reigned in the car, forcing itself on us as an unspoken command. I cradled Billy in my trembling arms in the back seat as the countryside rushed past. The triangular window at my right shoulder snapped images of harvesters on neighboring farms. Everyday life. Now everyday life was shattered.

Vera looked over at me. At eight years of age, my younger sister was as fun-loving as she was hard-working. Now her mouth quivered in an effort to keep back sobs that would distract Dad, her shaking hand awkwardly stroking Billy's tussled goldenrod hair. I returned her glance, and nodded. There was nothing to say; my mouth wouldn't form any words.

Billy's cornflower-blue eyes fluttered open and focused on mine.

"Owee, Nina. Owee." He gently moved his legs, as if trying to run away from the pain. I winced at his nickname for me.

I tightened my arms around him and refused to take my eyes off his face. Before I could form any words of comfort to him, Billy's eyes rolled back.

His body went limp.

Dawn to Dusk Duties

Chapter Three

Dad swung the Ford up to the emergency entrance of the hospital parking lot. Mom jumped out of the car just as it stopped, ran around the front, and jerked open my door. The cool autumn air rushed in as she scooped Billy from my arms and turned and ran into the hospital. Billy, though unconscious, looked fine; no blood stained his little body, no bruise or scrape belied an injury. My mind fought with my heart. Surely he would be alright. Dad quickly unfolded his tall frame from the car and directed his words to Vera and me.

"Wait here," he commanded.

Then he turned to catch up to Mom.

Mutely nodding, we watched as the double doors swallowed Mom, Dad, and Billy. Although we remained in the car, I felt my heart go right through those double doors with them. I felt hollow inside.

A long time passed.

Vera and I watched the cars come and go in the parking lot, shifting our position in the back seat of the car. We didn't speak; we simply wouldn't—or couldn't—allow the questions in our minds to form themselves into words.

I glanced out the window again. This time I saw the '52 Plymouth wagon belonging to my aunt and uncle pull up next to us. When they parked and opened the car door, I heard little Karen whimpering softly in Aunt Laurie's arms. Wordless, they tumbled awkwardly out of the car and hurried to the hospital entrance where they too were swallowed by the double doors.

Then we cried. And cried and cried.

And we waited. And waited and waited.

Doctors' offices and hospitals and emergency rooms represented a completely foreign culture to us. We had no idea what was going on behind those double doors or how long it would take. Our parents, expecting us to obey without question and to do so until further notice, knew where we were and we knew they would return to us when they could. Until then my younger sister and I, holding hands and weeping, now begged God repeatedly, "Whatever you do, God, don't let Billy die."

*****

His Ways Are Higher

Our home ran like clockwork. Arising early, we dressed quickly and went about our daily chores without much conversation, waking up more fully as we swept the floors, or set the table for breakfast. My folks generally delegated household tasks according to age and gender, teaching us once or twice what was expected and then leaving us alone. Indoor work—such as making supper, washing dishes and general cleaning or gardening—was inspected by Mom while Dad supervised outdoor chores related to the barnyard. I was "Chicken Boss" in the winter, and often helped toss hay to the cattle in the cold. We planted gardens in spring, baled hay and canned vegetables in summer, and harvested the bounty in fall. We girls helped make supper—most often potatoes, vegetables, and meat—every day. Saturday mornings were reserved for housecleaning, and we older ones always helped care for the younger ones—something I always enjoyed, partly because playing hide-and-seek provided a welcome break from scrubbing floors. Mom and Dad tolerated no disobedience and demanded excellence in all our work.

The week was loosely structured: wash clothes on Monday, iron clothes on Tuesday, mend clothes on Wednesday, clean house on Saturday.

Usually my folks didn't expect us to do many chores on weekdays before school because getting ready for the early-morning bus kept us busy enough. In the winter we breakfasted on porridge before the sun was up while Mom made peanut-butter-and-jelly sandwiches to put in our lunch pails. In autumn she sometimes treated us to fresh tomato or cucumber sandwiches—a real treat, we thought.

Our family of seven lived in a three-bedroom, one bath simple frame house. Because it was much larger than our previous home, no one complained about the extra maintenance. In fact it wasn't until we moved into this house that we had running water; prior to that we children did the running to get the water. A favorite amenity was an indoor flushing toilet—quite an upgrade from the outhouse that we had often used in 40-degree-below-zero winter weather.

Mom and Dad shared one room with a crib where Billy slept, Vi and I shared another, and the younger siblings shared the third bedroom. None of us expected to have the privilege of private quarters. Our small room housed a double bed, a dresser, and a small table where we studied our lessons. The small closet held the few necessary pieces of clothing we owned and, compared to our neighbors, we lived in extravagance.

*****

His Ways Are Higher

Finally Uncle George pushed open the hospital door. He waved to us to get our attention, then motioned for us to come in. Now we too were to be swallowed by those double doors.

Vera and I slipped out of the car and walked through those double doors, silently entering a world that held both death and life. The light-green walls in the hallway spoke to us of a sterile, sober environment. Nurses with clipboards in their hands walked by us as if we were invisible. Another set of closed double doors marked the emergency room where Billy lay.

We made our way to the metal chairs lining the walls. Vera and I looked at each other again, and waited.

Then we heard them—great, heaving, broken sobs.

I turned in the direction of the familiar voice. My mother, having just come through those double doors of the emergency room, now held a tissue to her mouth, desperately trying to hold back the heart-wrenching cries that exploded from the depths of her being.

Impulsively I ran to her. Throwing my arms around her quaking shoulders, I hugged her for all I was worth, hoping somehow to stop the pain flowing out of her soul by pressing my own body against hers.

It couldn't be...No! It couldn't be...

I drew back and looked into her blurred, deep blue eyes overflowing with grief. I whispered the question that I really didn't want answered.

"Has Billy gone to heaven?"

Mom nodded, and my own heart ripped in two.

Life and Death

Chapter Four

I fell into Mom's arms, sobbing. Her own heaving gasps for breath and uncontrolled weeping told me she was as bewildered as I. *Billy could not be gone—he simply couldn't be! He was toddling about only a few hours ago.*

A lady, garbed in a starched white nurse's uniform, brought each of us a glass of water and a pill.

"A sedative," she said quietly. I obediently swallowed the water and the pill, sank into a brown vinyl chair that had been pushed against the wall and, with my head in my hands, wept quietly. My world had fallen in all around me, and I was absolutely thunderstruck.

After awhile I felt a strong but gentle hand on my shoulder. I looked up into the face of Billy's doctor. I could see sorrow in his eyes, too, but I also saw kindness. He cleared his throat and spoke in a hushed tone.

"You're a strong girl, Linda."

Later, after the endless drive home, the sedative began to take effect. I stumbled through the door to my room and fell on my bed. Just before sleep overcame me, clouded thoughts shot through my head.

Billy is gone! Billy is gone!

*****

Our family attended *Nordheim Mennonite Church* every Sunday morning. Arising early, we completed our chores, inhaled bowls of cereal, and rushed off the three-quarters of a mile on foot to the modest white clapboard building that was ornamented only with a plywood sign out front.

I loved going to church. The Sunday service not only provided a welcome break from weekday routines; it also held the weekly treat of Bible stories, enhanced by six days of growing anticipation. While the Sunday-school teacher talked, I sat forward intently, Bible open in my lap, feet wrapped around the wooden chair legs. I listened carefully. As I heard an old story, my mind vividly painted a picture of a young boy with only a few fish and loaves of bread. I imagined five thousand hungry people sitting on a greening hillside, and then in my mind's eye I saw Jesus blessing the young boy's lunch.

I could just *see* all those hungry men, women, and children eating those fish and wiping bread crumbs from their mouths. *Indeed*, I agreed in my heart, *this was a miracle*.

I was amazed that this story could be a historical reality. My heart yearned to know more about this carpenter of Galilee, to know if He really rose from the dead and was alive today, but I wasn't sure how to grow in that knowledge.

Mom was a great help, answering my questions and reviewing scripture verses with me when I came home from a neighborhood Good News Club. She even took the time, busy as she was, to go through a Bible correspondence course with me.

When I was ten, all that I had heard about faith seemed to come together and I knew I didn't want to only know *about* Jesus; I wanted to *know* Him personally.

One night our family attended a crusade about forty miles away. The pastor spoke from John 3:16, the Bible verse that talks about God loving us so much that He gave His only Son so that we could experience eternal life. I could not imagine any parent being willing to give up his child. That would simply be too much heartache. Such love was unfathomable.

Linda A. Olson

When I heard that Jesus willingly died on the cross, even when he had done nothing wrong, for the ultimate purpose of our being forgiven for our sins, I was deeply moved. The pastor mentioned verses found in Romans 6 that tell us about sin and death, and he spoke of the opportunity available to us to have eternal life, to live with God forever.

I didn't understand all that he said that December evening, but I did grasp that God loved me very much, and I felt something stirring deep within me. This is what I had been hungering for. This is what I wanted. When the pastor invited anyone who would like to pray to receive the Lord to come forward, I quickly bowed my head to avoid eye contact with him. Then I peeked to see if anyone was getting up. Suddenly I knew I was more interested in my own response than in anyone else's.

With my heart pounding, I quietly stood and moved past my sister to the center aisle. I raised my head, took a deep breath, and walked toward the front of the church. I would receive Christ.

A woman with a gentle smile asked me to follow her. She led me to a quiet prayer room where she shared with me that this was the most important decision I would ever make. She prayed for me, and then I spoke my own words to the Lord, asking Him to come into my life. The woman smiled again and suggested

30

His Ways Are Higher

I write the date in the front of my Bible to remind me of the day I made the decision to accept God's free gift of salvation.

With great inner rejoicing I did just that. Taking the black pen she extended to me, I carefully wrote on the flyleaf of my black leatherette Bible, "December 2, 1962. I accepted Jesus as my Lord and Savior."

It was a long ride home. All was quiet. We were wrapped in the warmth of our heavy winter coats against the cold December air. I knew the events of the evening were familiar to my family—many of them had previously received the Lord—but, for some reason, no one spoke to me about my life-changing decision. Here my heart was bursting with joy at this new experience, and no one celebrated with me. I knew our people weren't very demonstrable when it came to expressing faith, but the lack of interest only seemed to intensify my natural loneliness.

The next morning, arising early to bundle up for the walk to school, I made my brother and sister promise they wouldn't tell anyone at school about the decision I had made the night before. I wasn't exactly ashamed, but I didn't want to get teased either. And because I had always gone to church and had been a fairly compliant child, obeying easily with a sincere desire to do right, my outward behavior simply didn't change much after my prayer that night. However, on the inside, I was flooded with inexpressible peace accompanied by an even deeper hunger to serve Him.

My relationship with Christ deepened daily. I was sent weekly lessons of instruction in biblical doctrine, and I faithfully completed each one, licking the stamp and affixing it to the long white envelope with satisfaction before I dropped it in the mail. When I finished the course, I was given a little book as a reward for my diligent work. The lessons helped temper the do's and don'ts uniquely associated with our church culture, and I found my new relationship with Jesus to be the beginning of a most treasured friendship. I knew even more clearly that He was with me always.

*****

Dad quietly opened the bedroom door. The sun, already shining through my window, made me squint as I struggled to rise from the deep sleep caused by the sedative. Slowly the memory of a terrible nightmare surfaced in my consciousness. Surely it was a nightmare, a terrible dream, one of those that just *seems* frighteningly real. Billy was still sleeping in the next bedroom, just like always, wasn't he?

With great effort, I focused my eyes on my father's face, his own eyes dark and swollen. Standing in the doorway, his six-foot frame was now bent over as if he had no strength to stand straight. Dad's eyes were filled with tears. No, the nightmare was real. *Billy was gone. Our Billy was gone.*

He swallowed, and our eyes met briefly. "We've got to get up; we've got to keep going," he said.

I just looked at him, my own eyes brimming over. I had no idea how in the world we were going to keep going. Slowly Dad nodded at me and backed out of the doorway, quietly turning the brass doorknob. As he pulled the door closed, the latch clicking into the doorjamb, I wondered if the door of my heart had also just swung shut, latching into a place that would protect me from the incredible, almost palpable pain that was tearing it apart.

Mom

Chapter Five

We sat together in the living room, silent. Another knock.

I glanced at Mom, waited for her nearly-imperceptible nod, and rose to open the screen door. The large wooden door that had once protected us from the harsh world outside no longer existed, having been crushed by the tractor. Relatives stood on what was left of the porch, their faces draped in sadness. I invited them in, automatically taking from them the casserole they held with hot pads. Numbly I carried it to the kitchen and set it on the stove beside two other covered dishes. All this food, but who could eat?

Who could eat without Billy at the table? Would any of us ever eat again?

My thoughts continued on a downward spiral. Then, like she could read my thoughts, my mother's cousin looked at me and gently spoke.

"The sun will shine again for you some day," she whispered.

I nodded politely, but my heart shook its refusal to believe the audacious statement. *How could the sun ever shine again?* All around me was darkness.

We received word that little Karen was not doing well. Her injuries required more specialized care and she had been transported to a hospital in Winnipeg, two hundred and fifty miles away. Not yet out of the woods, she was scheduled for emergency surgery to repair a ruptured kidney.

When I realized that Karen too might not make it, my traumatized faith suddenly came rushing back to me. Where I had held God at arm's length during the few days immediately following Billy's death, I no longer could stand the distance between us. I was crumbling inside, and I loved little Karen.

And I loved God. Only He knew how to knit her back together. Surely he would spare her life, wouldn't He? Indeed, I realized He was our only hope for Karen. I began to silently beg the Lord.

Please, God! I can't take two deaths. Don't take her, too.

My heart, already shredded by the loss of Billy, was barely beating in my benumbed body. If Karen died, would I ever draw another breath myself?

As a family, we poured our grief over losing Billy into prayers for Karen's healing. I knew that—like it or not—I could no longer keep God away from my pain.

His Ways Are Higher

To intentionally reject Him was to reject any possibility of healing, both healing of Karen and healing of our heartache.

*****

Grandma and Grandpa Warkentin, my mother's parents, emigrated from Russia to Canada in the mid 1920's. Life had been hard for the Russian Mennonites, so they decided to bring their three young children (Mom hadn't been born yet) across the ocean for a fresh start. Settling in Southern Manitoba, the family welcomed my mother in 1927. A few years later, they moved to Winnipegosis. Soon another daughter joined the family, and then twins were born (although only one survived). Shortly afterward, Grandmother broke her hip. With limited medical help available, she would never again walk without crutches.

Mom grew up steeped in the faith of her parents, completing a seventh grade education but never fulfilling her dream of completing high school. Shy and inhibited, she nevertheless accepted the hardworking role of a middle child, helping her older siblings with chores every day as well as tending to the needs of her younger sisters.

The Mennonite culture emphasizes hard work, loyalty, commitment, and perseverance. What it did not emphasize in my mother's day was any open expression of affection. Somehow love permeated the family, but spoken words of affirmation and approval were few and far between. A hug here or a peck on the cheek there were rare occurrences. Mom, having grown up without these physical affirmations, carried the reserved behavior into her own family when she married and, except for obvious touching necessary for babies and toddlers, she expressed her love toward her own children through acts of service—sewing dresses for us girls, baking favorite desserts for my brother.

The church reinforced this stoic behavior. Legalistic by historical nature, the elders in the church modeled a way of life nearly void of emotion. Public worship was demonstrated in services by bowed heads during prayer and open hymnbooks during singing. Private worship included saying grace before meals and following the Ten Commandments as much as possible so we could be "doers of the word and not hearers only". We talked only when necessary, with most conversations reserved for mealtimes.

Any outward sign of emotion was frowned upon and seen as an outburst to be controlled. After the accident, we rarely expressed our grief. Days were long and lonely. Sometimes, unable to reconcile the reality of Billy's absence, we lashed out at one another with sharp and hurtful accusations. Communication, difficult before, now bordered on the nearly impossible.

His Ways Are Higher

Mom had always been my confidante and trusted teacher, but soon she drifted into her own world of hurt. Consumed by the tragedy, she simply backed away from relationship with any of us, speaking only when necessary, and then only when chores were left undone or schoolwork was due. Often, I glanced at her as she bent over the mending or when she stood at the sink washing dishes, watching her face visibly harden, her mouth squeeze tight into a thin line. She seemed as if she were trying with all her might to shut out the horrific memory of the day when she lost her little boy. She simply couldn't see that we were grieving too. In many ways, I began to feel a double loss: Billy my beloved brother, and Mom my beloved teacher.

As news of the accident spread, neighbors called and relatives brought more food. Friends sent cards, and everyone helped where they could. But after the customary bereavement period, the church community did little to console our family. Too soon, the knocks on the door ceased and questions about our wellbeing evaporated. Our home rarely saw a visitor and grief closed in, silent and dark. No one talked with us. No one cried with us. No one asked if we were alright.

No one checked on us to see how we were dealing with the unbearable pain that continued to tighten around us like a tourniquet, squeezing us so hard we could barely breathe.

And no one came to listen as we searched our faith for answers.

*****

Always, tragedy and death force questions about eternity into the front and center position of everyday life. *Where was God in all this? How could He let this happen to a sweet, innocent baby? How do we get through the next moment, the next supper, the next birthday?* We didn't voice our bewilderment then, but perhaps we would have if someone would have asked. Instead, we felt alone in our own dark valley of despair. Our family's collective heart had been broken, divided among Mom and Dad, my siblings and myself. Now it lay in pieces in the awareness that we would never again hear Billy sing *"Kumbaya, Lord"*, never again feel his chubby arms wrap around our necks before he went to bed, and never again glimpse his overalls as he ran out the front door, screen door slamming behind him, to greet whoever drove onto our gravel driveway to visit.

*****

His Ways Are Higher

I stood with my family at the back of the church, pressing my feet into the floor for all I was worth, shifting my weight. *How could I make it through this day?*

The funeral director turned and motioned us to follow him. Two by two, I and my brother and sisters walked behind our parents as we were ushered down the center aisle. Awkwardly we filed into the first few rows of seats. Neighbors, friends, relatives, and acquaintances packed our little church for Billy's funeral. I sat, knowing that someone was speaking, hearing a voice, but I was unable to comprehend the words. Surely this was all a dream, a nightmare. I would wake up soon and Billy would run to me for his morning hug.

Eventually the voice stopped. Other voices, now hushed in the aftermath of the service, spoke hollow words of comfort. Someone patted my shoulder. When all the words had been said and all of the patting had stopped, I watched as the people slowly made their way to the back courtyard, leaving the pews empty.

I slowly walked to the front of the church where the body of my precious little brother lay. I peered into the coffin, realizing with mixed feelings of pain and wonder that Billy was not there. The lifeless form, still and pale, silently declared the end of my relationship with him on earth, yet I knew that Billy—the *real* Billy—was alive and well somewhere else. Still, as the funeral director began to close the coffin, I suddenly panicked, impulsively grabbing the director's arm. I wanted to scream, *"No, don't close the coffin! Don't close the coffin on Billy!"*

Instead I bowed my head and sobbed.

Silent Sorrow

Chapter Six

I took my gray sweater from the hook in my locker and slammed the metal door shut. English class started in two minutes and, although I was eager to escape the deafening silence at home, I also dreaded the inevitable return to school. News traveled fast among two hundred fifty students, and this morning I felt every single one of them was staring at me with accusation.

She's the one who killed her brother. I could hear their unspoken taunts.

"I didn't see you in school last week; is everything alright?" Startled, I looked around to see who had spoken. Luna, my dark-haired, brown-eyed classmate, shifted her books to her other arm and waited for my response. Fresh pain seared through me again, and I had no words to answer her. *How could anything ever be alright again?* Not trusting my voice, I simply nodded in mute assent—completely denying that everything was alright—and we walked to class. Would the day never end?

Linda A. Olson

The days turned into weeks. I talked only during class when an answer or recitation was required. Small talk during our breaks evaded me, and I often ate alone, uneasy with normal teenage bantering. My cousin Lila soon began to invite me to join her and her friend during the long, lonely lunch hours. That helped tremendously. After several weeks I felt comfortable enough to walk with them down Main Street, picking up a snack and chatting about everyday happenings. The normalcy of life gradually began to return, helping me put one foot in front of another despite the agony of Billy's absence in our home.

One afternoon I sat in class, oblivious to what the teacher was saying. My mind refused to focus on page numbers and chapter headings.

"No assignment this morning, Linda?" Mrs. Hrushowy, kind but firm, glanced at my bowed head and blank paper.

I looked up and shook my head. With one swift glance, she took in my red and swollen eyes, my fidgeting hands, my shuffling feet. I was holding my breath, ashamed of my scattered thinking. I waited for the rebuke. But she smiled gently, patted my arm, and marked an "X" in her assignment book next to my name. Relieved and ever-so-grateful, I let out my breath. "X" meant "excused".

*****

His Ways Are Higher

Losing Billy to death was hard enough, but not knowing what to do with the intense emotional pain caused by the circumstances of his death only compounded the grief. No one in my family had even heard about professional counselors and back then we were unaware of grief support groups. Consequently, even in the deepest of sorrow, tears were forced back and conversation, when not harsh and irritating, was stilted and polite among us. After Billy died, especially when the funeral was over and the necessary work on the farm resumed—and that was within days of his burial—his death was rarely mentioned again. Our unexpressed grief became intensely private, trapped inside each parent, each sibling, and each extended relative with no way of acceptable escape. Mom, especially, didn't reveal the brokenness of her own heart after the tragedy. Tending to the house, her husband, and her other children, she mechanically moved her body through breakfast, lunch, and supper. Dutifully she maintained her position as wife and mother, but her tender spirit began to evaporate, dissipating into the silent cavern of our home, now void of Billy's playful chatter. She didn't seem to realize she no longer laughed.

She simply just ceased to smile.

*****

Linda A. Olson

My parents desperately tried to find a way to fill the empty hole in their lives that Billy left. They hurt. Of course they hurt. We all hurt. Each one of us felt the dull ache that refused to let go. One day Mom, licking the flap on an envelope, gave me a letter to mail.

"Be careful with this, Linda, and don't forget to pick up any mail to bring home." Her monotone voice, like the unchanging ticking of a clock, simply reminded me of my role as the family mail carrier. I loved the every-day opportunity during my lunch hour at school to walk to and from the post office. Breathing in the smell of roses and looking at sunflowers nodding their heads in the afternoon light brought a small measure of balm to my aching soul. This particular spring day, just before I dropped the letter into the mail slot, I noticed that Mom's neat handwriting spelled out the address of an adoption agency. I was taken aback, shaken with a sense of betrayal.

Were they trying to replace Billy with another child? My heart sank, not because I would not welcome another baby in the house, but because such a life-changing decision had not even been mentioned to us children. We were simply expected to abide by whatever decisions my parents made, regardless of how they affected us. My eyes blurred with tears as I sank even further into the abyss of grief, knowing that the ever-present message at home was that personal matters were never discussed.

His Ways Are Higher

The adoption never went through. Instead, eighteen months after the accident, we gladly took turns sharing Mom's chores after she delivered a new baby girl into the family circle. The attending doctor spoke aloud to my father the words that were silently humming in each of our hearts that spring morning.

"It's a good thing this is a girl because no one could ever replace your son."

He was right.

*****

My thoughts often wandered to the precious moments with Billy.

"Nina," Billy called. I loved his nickname for me. We, along with my twelve-year-old brother Len, and sisters Vi and Vera, were herding together the cows, newborn calves and bulls. Our job every spring was to drive them to a distant pasture several miles away where they would graze all summer. For me, herding the cattle was simply an annual routine. For Billy, a toddler only just beginning to talk in complete sentences, it was a new adventure. I carried a stick with me, ready to redirect any cow who thought charging me might be a good idea. But Billy had been learning the ropes of herding from Len. With great authority, the little boy came up to me, demonstrating his approach. "Nina, you have to wave your arms so the cows will see you!" he called to me. I chuckled at his enthusiasm.

No fear for this young man.

"Why?"

Chapter Seven

"Hey, Linda! We're going on a hayride! Want to come?" Daryl shouted to me as he grabbed his jacket from our hall peg.

A friend to my cousin Lila, Daryl and two guys and two gals had accompanied Lila on the three-hundred-mile drive from the small Bible College in Manitoba. A long weekend had afforded enough time for the students to visit with our extended family and, although they were a few years my senior, they included me easily in their plans for several days. They knew of Billy's accident and were surprisingly sensitive to the reluctance I exhibited in making friends.

"Sure, Linda, why don't you come? We're going to sing a few songs on the ride and then come back to Klassens's house for some hot chocolate." Lila spoke with genuine enthusiasm. Always quick to include me, she and her classmates were friendly and fun and excited about having personal relationship with Christ. When they visited us, they joined eagerly with the family in the Sunday morning services by singing or giving testimony. Never pretending to be professional singers or speakers, they nonetheless spoke sincerely, their words coming from the heart. Clearly, something drew me to them. I also noticed an excitement in my cousin I had not seen before. She seemed to enjoy life so much. What I would give for that!

I responded impulsively. "Sure, I'll come, if Mom says I may. Be right there!"

I ran to get my sweater. I could hardly wait to climb up onto the hayrack.

*****

Everyday life since Billy's death settled into a blur of daily chores and schoolwork and weekly Sunday meetings. The accident was never mentioned, but no one forgot the little boy who had brought such sunshine into our lives.

Our family recalled two incidents that occurred just a month or so before Billy died. Our neighbors had retired to a Senior Care Home in our small town. Occasionally they would bring an elderly friend from the home to our house to enjoy an afternoon on the farm. This time they brought someone we had never met. The elderly man was not able to walk well, so he remained in the car with the door open while he enjoyed the energy and enthusiasm of little Billy entertaining him for hours with his antics on the driveway. The man later commented to Dad, "This boy will not live to see old age."

Alarmed at his remark, Dad questioned him. "Why do you say that?"

The old man smiled just a bit and looked again at Billy as the toddler bent over to examine a bug in the garden. "He's too good for this earth. I have 90 grandchildren and not one of them is like this one."

Another time Dad gathered several neighbors to help him hang the door on our huge machine shed. Since it had recently rained, the men were ankle-deep in mud. Billy, always in the thick of things, wanted to be part of the action. Playing nearby, he was determined to help however he could. But, at one point, the door began to slip. The men could not get their footing in the mud and the door began to turn, its massive weight shifting out of their hands. When the men could no longer hold the falling door, Dad yelled at the top of his lungs. "Billy, get out of the way!"

Like a shot, Billy immediately took off running. The huge door fell with a muddy splash, right on the footprints where Billy had stood just seconds before. Silence reigned for a few moments as the men realized a tragedy had just been narrowly averted.

With Billy's death came questions, so many questions. Questions about life, about Billy, about me. I especially was tormented by questions about the accident. *Why did God allow it to happen? Why didn't He stop it?* And my biggest question remained.

Why was I the one on the tractor that took his life that day?

Since I could find no answers, and I had no one to talk to about them, I buried myself in what I *could* do: housework and schoolwork. But I also studied my Bible, and one day I read a passage that seemed to speak just to me.

'For My thoughts are not your thoughts, Nor are your ways My ways,' says the Lord. For as the heavens are higher than the earth, So are My ways higher than your ways, And My thoughts than your thoughts (Isaiah 55:8, 9 NKJV).

That settled it. I still had questions, but after I read that passage, I somehow felt an unmistakable peace. I knew it was unlikely my questions would be answered this side of Heaven, yet God had given me an assurance that His ways were best even when I didn't understand. Beneath all the guilt and hurt, I knew He was there. Surely I had no idea when I was ten years old that my simple prayer had laid the spiritual foundation for the rest of my life. In time I found a verse that became my personal cornerstone.

His Ways Are Higher

Because I had searched and searched for answers, these words became my own private treasure.

"God decided to let his people know this rich and glorious secret that He has for all people. This secret is Christ himself, who is in you. He is our only hope for glory" Colossians 1:27 (NCV).

I realized then that, if God was who He said He was, I would have to believe His Word. With a childlike faith I hung on to this treasure, my own personal promise. It was the only hope I had. Since God had known the accident would happen and allowed such devastation to come into my life, I could only wonder. *Could this really be part of His bigger plan?*

*****

After high school several close friends and relatives strongly encouraged me to attend Winnipeg Bible College, even if it was for only a year. I honestly didn't know if I would fit in. Everyone I had met seemed talented and outgoing, and I frankly didn't know if I could handle the academics. Could I really keep my mind on my studies? Could I forget the accident enough to really apply myself to a rigorous schedule of classes, homework, and tests?

*****

Linda A. Olson

In those days, a girl seemingly had only three career choices: become a secretary, a nurse, or a teacher. Secretarial work sounded boring, and I had never been attracted to the medical field. The only option that was even a possibility was becoming a teacher. When I was sixteem I had taught five weeks of Vacation Bible School for five-year-olds, and I had absolutely loved it. The thought of becoming a kindergarten teacher raised my interest, but I didn't know if I was ready to go to University.

Since neither of my parents completed grade school because of family hardships, education simply was not a high value in our home. When I expressed interest in college, Dad made it clear that he would not be able to help financially. The twenty-five dollars I had saved over the summer (money earned by working with my brother and sister pitching eleven hundred bales of hay a day) would not even cover the cost of gas to get to the school. My thoughts swirled. *What do I do? I don't even know where to turn.* Fear began to rise up in me—the now-familiar heart-squeezing, head-throbbing fear. If anything kept me from attending college, it would be just that: fear. Fear of failure, fear of not being able to fit in, fear of not meeting my financial commitment. But, most of all, I was consumed with the fear of what the students and faculty would think of me if they learned about the accident. *How could anyone with my background succeed at anything, let alone college?*

Again I turned the pages of my Bible, hunting, searching for what the Lord would say to me. *Ah! Here it is!* God was faithful to assure me of His care.

"He shall cover you with His feathers, And under His wings you shall take refuge; His truth shall be your shield and buckler" Psalm 91:4 (NKJV)

*****

I picked out the long white business envelope from the stack of mail and read the return address: Winnipeg Bible College. *This was it. Either I'm in or I'm not.* I grasped the other envelopes tightly, putting the letter from the college on the bottom of the stack—somehow guarding its privacy—and pushed open the heavy steel door of the post office. I wanted to read the news privately and so I headed to the nearby maple trees, Anxious, I sat on the boulder at the base of the maple tree and uttered a brief silent prayer.

Lord, prepare my heart. Then I tore open the envelope.

"Mom! Dad!" I shouted before I even reached the entryway. "Mom! Dad! I'm in! I've been accepted at Winnipeg Bible College!" I burst into the kitchen.

They turned to me, Mom set down the butter on the table and Dad dried his hands on the kitchen towel.

"Well", Dad said, "That's good." He said no more, but that was enough. I knew it was his way of saying he supported me.

Thanks-giving

Chapter Eight

What had I been thinking? I stared at the paper in front of me. *I've only been here three weeks and I can't even finish the assignment. What made me think I could make it in college?* I sat under the maple tree, its golden leaves sparkling in the September sunshine. I was to write a paper on my personal strengths and weaknesses.

I groaned inwardly. I had the weakness part down, all right. The list of attributes that I looked on as drawbacks extended nearly to the end of the paper. But strengths? With *my* background? Who was I kidding? Whoever would think that an ordinary farm girl who just tried to obey what she was asked to do had any strengths? I had never considered that I possibly *had* any strengths. Anyone could do what I did. There wasn't anything special about me.

I felt caught between a rock and a hard place. Watching students get into cars and drive off-campus, I realized that, if I had been offered a ride back home, I would have jumped at the opportunity.

Anything to get away from the academic challenges I was facing.

But it was a fleeting thought. The next thought addressed the flip-side of that temptation. *What is there at home that would make me stay there?* I realized that in our small farming community of 500 people, only folks who inherited family farms stayed there. Nearly every other young adult left their parents to find careers of their own. A familiar phrase flitted across my mind: "Once you leave your comfort zone, it is no longer comfortable." Sighing, I picked up my Bible.

*****

Dealing with the death of a loved one provides opportunity for incredibly hard emotional work. Sorrow comes in waves, overcoming and ever-coming at unexpected times. I would be seated in class, diligently listening to a lecture, and a picture of Billy would flash across my mind. By the time I had realized once again that his death had occurred because of something I had done, I would momentarily drown in sorrow and then consciously have to reel myself in, putting intense mental energy into switching my thoughts to the present lecture. I forced myself to pay attention to the words of the professor. Yet even then, I would sometimes miss vital information in those few moments when Billy occupied my thoughts. Often it was not the guilt associated with the death of my little brother that overwhelmed me; it was simply the natural sorrow of knowing I would never see him again this side of heaven, never watch him grow up, never again tuck him into bed at night.

This, of course, played havoc with my spiritual life. My parents did not blame me for Billy's death, nor did my brother or sisters. My family knew absolutely that I had not been negligent or cocky at the wheel of the tractor. Farming accidents occurred regularly in the community and, although tragic, crops still had to be planted and harvested if the remaining family was to eat in the winter. Only at college did I have the opportunity to escape the daily fight for survival and purposefully glimpse through a window into the future.

One day in chapel, a guest speaker issued a challenge: "*In everything give thanks.*" These words, taken from I Thessalonians 5:16-18, caused a wrestling match in my heart.

How could I thank God for taking little Billy? I had pushed most of my questions aside, satisfied to leave the unanswerable to God alone. Yet that foundational question resurfaced in my mind: *Why was I the one driving the tractor that killed my brother?* Then the questions dominoed. *Why couldn't I have died instead of him? He was only two-*

and-a-half! Why was his life cut short and not mine? Yet it seemed as if God Himself, through the guest speaker, was giving me a solid command to give thanks.

How in the world can I do that, Lord? Especially since I was responsible for the accident?

This concept proved to be difficult on another level. My anxieties about school had thankfully begun to dissipate. Like a flower bud that opens in spring, I began to blossom in my new life away from home. I hungrily drank in new rays of friendships and I found roots growing deeper into the spiritual soil of my relationship with God. My days, not only filled with classes and homework, now brimmed with laughter, snowball fights, ping-pong tournaments, dorm raids, dates, and banquets. My self-confidence soared as I ventured into new opportunities each semester.

Yet, contrasted with this budding new life, I still had to deal with the confines of my life at home. I simply could not shake off the reality that I had killed Billy, however unintended. I desired peace, profound peace, in the deepest of places in my soul, but those places seemed remote, unreachable. Places where laughter and good times couldn't reach.

My heart beat dully. I turned automatically to my little brother in conversation. *Oh, Billy, I am so sorry I hurt you. I wish so much that I would have gone to heaven now instead of you. You deserved to live a good, long life. Maybe if you had lived and I had died, neither one of us would be hurting...*

With great effort, I pulled my thoughts back to my assignment. Tomorrow I was to give my testimony in front of my classmates, and I was terrified. The familiar fear of rejection *(What will my friends think of me?)* now was accompanied by confusion *(Why did I ever agree to this?)* and I simply could not comprehend how I could make it through the oral presentation. Yet I felt an unfamiliar urgency in my spirit: this was something I needed to do, something I *must* do.

I folded my arms on my desk and buried my face. I had come to a decision.

Oh, Lord, I prayed. *Please help me with this assignment. I don't understand why I should thank you for the accident, for Billy's death, for allowing his death to come through something that I did. But you tell me to thank you anyway. So, simply because you tell me to, I thank you. I thank you that, in the midst of my sorrow, You are here. I thank you that Billy is with You and that he isn't in any pain. And I thank you that I will see him again one day. Thank you, too, for holding my life in Your hands. I know You love me and have my best in mind. And I know You hurt when I hurt and that You care. The fact of Billy's death is never going to go away, and I must be able to talk about it. Lord, please help me in my own sorrow and my own search and give me the right words to say during chapel tomorrow, to say what I need to say. In Jesus' name, Amen.*

*****

"Linda," my friend told me after my talk. "That was great! You have been through so much! I'm so glad you told us about the accident. We're so sorry to hear about your little brother, and we want you to know we'll be praying for you. Anytime you want to talk, we're here."

I was astonished.

Far from the rejection that I had expected, I now saw a circle of friends I could talk with and cry with. I sensed their genuine support. This turning point for me, this emotional breakthrough, marked the beginning of my healing.

Patterns

Chapter Nine

I sighed as I put the dust cloth on the hook of the cleaning cart. *Will I ever be able to afford to stay in a nice hotel where someone else makes my bed and scrubs my bathroom?*

As a summer maid at a local hotel, I quickly learned how to make a snug bed and polish a bathroom until it shone. My friends often shared with me their dreams for the future, but I realized I didn't share my dreams with them. And that was because I seldom had dreams to share. *Dreams? What dreams?* I didn't have any dreams. I didn't even know what it was like to dream. I had studied books, given presentations, passed tests, and made it through my first year of college.

Yet, here I was, scrubbing toilets and running a vacuum cleaner. I was thrilled for a summer job, but this only met a temporary and necessary financial need. My heart, heavy with discouragement, pleaded with my mind. *Will I ever have the courage to dream big dreams?*

Crisis of any kind rattles the bones of everyday existence. Although my time at college brimmed with assignments and activities, the ever-present buried accusations pushed their way to the surface unexpectedly, especially during times of solitude. Often, right before I lay my head on the pillow at night, I would hear the relentless thoughts. *Will I ever have the confidence to do something besides scrubbing toilets the rest of my life? I must be extra-careful so I don't ever cause another accident, Will I ever get past this?* Overwhelming, continual grief had eventually subsided to a dull heartache—a bitter recipe of remorse, questions, guilt, and simply missing Billy.

I had done everything I knew to do, putting one foot in front of another, day by day, yet something was still missing. I felt disqualified from being a dreamer. Somehow, I reasoned, since I cut short Billy's life, I must also cut short my own hopes and dreams for a fulfilling future. *If Billy can't have dreams,* I reasoned, *then neither can I.* The internal discussion rarely rested. Years later I read a quote by Bruce Wilkinson:"The way of the Dreamer is difficult—but anything less is hardly worth living at all!" I wanted to dream big, I really did. But could I? Was I "allowed" to? I began to review my life in light of the previous years.

His Ways Are Higher

First I looked at my own yearnings. Somehow I felt, deep down inside that I *was* made for something more than just going to school and working as a maid. But how did that square with my mind telling me I didn't deserve it? Had I learned anything in the past several years that could help me figure out how dreams could become reality? Were dreams even possible for someone like me?

Incident by incident, sitting quietly before the Lord in unspoken prayer, I began to review my first year at college. What was I missing? What was the common thread in my experiences? Was a specific direction already in place that would move me forward into my destiny?

After much waiting and introspection and listening, I found what seemed to be a regular pattern: I would be presented with a challenge that was inevitably accompanied by an initial fear of failure. After asking the Lord for wisdom and guidance, I would resolutely move into the experience with embryonic courage. Nearly always I came through the new challenge successfully, thereby building confidence that I was indeed able to overcome my fear.

Excitedly I reviewed more memories.Yes! The pattern held! The common thread was my obedience paired with God's faithfulness. I recognized that, no matter what the situation had been, I was presented with a choice. When I chose to do what I thought the

Lord was asking me to do, I came through the circumstance recognizing that God had been with me through the challenge. Eventually I saw with great relief that I would never go back to being the kind of person I was when I was fourteen. Billy's early demise did not have to be the shackles of an unfruitful life for *me.* My part in the accident was *not* an emotional prison sentence. I began to realize that those who knew me best really did forgive me for my part in Billy's death, and I found myself relaxing just the slightest bit in my own self-condemnation. My growing dreams reflected God's word in I Corinthians 2:9 *"No eye has seen, no ear has heard, no mind has conceived what God has prepared for those who love him" (NIV)*. My soul rejoiced, big time.

*****

" Linda! Why did you bring us out here? We're going to die!" Lula, just twelve years old, sat behind me in the canoe and put the paddle across her lap, inadvertently splashing me. Her voice trembled as she screamed at me, "Why did you even make us come out here?"

I squinted at the sky, ignoring her question. Obvious scorn and accusation did nothing to help the situation. Dark clouds were rolling in from the west, and I was more than a little concerned about our safety.

Why, indeed? After receiving an invitation to become an intern for a year at Youth for Christ, I jumped into being part of a "big sister" type of program. To my utter astonishment I was soon asked to be Director—and I was only twenty years old! My responsibilities included coordinating seventy-five volunteers with their "little sisters" while planning activities and Bible Studies and directing summer camps.

Today I was leading nine girls on a three-day canoeing adventure. And what an adventure it was turning out to be!

I glanced anxiously at the girls in the other canoes. Did they see the ominous clouds? Feel the change in the weather? I could hear their complaints above the rising shrill of the wind, their adolescent voices insulting each other. Most of the girls, angry at life, simply gave up if a task was too difficult. And, unbelievably, they didn't seem to care if they succeeded or failed, if they lived or died. Failure had become part of their expected everyday existence.

The wind bit into me. The unexpected storm white capped the water, rocking the canoe. What had started as a simple ride around the islands now turned into an emergency. If Lula didn't pick up her paddle and literally pull her own weight, we could be blown a long way from shore, with nothing in the canoe but light windbreakers and life jackets, and no way to signal for help. Again I wondered. *Did I really hear from God?*

I yelled over my shoulder, putting as much authority into my voice as I could muster. "Lula, put your paddle back in the water and pull—*hard*!" Indeed, I knew that I did not have the physical strength required to turn the canoe alone into the wind to head for shore. Silently I cried out. *God, please help us!*

I pulled my paddle into a j-stroke, kicking the end of the short, broad-bladed oar into a curve at the end of the pull. The water stung my eyes. Relieved, I saw Lula put her paddle back in the water, her back straightening as she leaned forward. Silently we pulled, intuitively matching our strokes. Blisters began to well up on my hands under the wooden handle. Veins stood out on my arms as I threw the wooden tool into the swells again and again, leaning and pulling, pressing the water backward. Pull. Kick it outward. Pull. Kick it outward.

Come! On! I told the canoe. *You! Must! Turn!* I repositioned my knees, rubbed raw against the wooden frame of the boat. Would the narrow craft obey my relentless command? Another stroke. Another. Another. Together now. Pull. *Pull!* I was breathing heavily. Throw the paddle; pull. Throw the paddle; pull!

Slowly, ever so slowly, the bow moved a few degrees to the left. *Throw the paddle; pull! Throw the paddle; pull!* The words took on the rhythmic beat of a song in my mind. *Throw the paddle; pull!* A few more degrees. Plunge the paddle into the water, brace the knees, and *pull!* More turning. *Pull! Pull! Pull!* I told myself. *Keep going!*

At last the canoe was headed in the direction of camp. "Pull hard, Lula! Pull hard!" I yelled into the wind, knowing that Lula and I must paddle in unison, repeatedly, determinedly.

I sat straighter, rolled my shoulders back, and threw the paddle into the water again. What should have been a thirty-minute pleasant ride had turned into hours of backbreaking work to slice the choppy water to get back to camp. Finally, my arms stinging and trembling, the canoe scraped pebbles in the shallow shoreline. I hopped from the bow into the cool water and, following my lead, Lula leaned back and threw her feet over the stern. We grabbed the gunwales and heaved the canoe up on to the beach, clear of any possibility of tidewater washing it back into the lake.

I looked around. Amazingly, the other canoes weren't far behind us. I did a quick head-count. All were present and accounted for. I let out my breath.

Thank You. Lord. Utterly relieved and spent, I stopped for a moment to gather my thoughts. The girls would be outraged at me.

But the voices of the girls weren't angry. Instead, I detected an unexpected excitement in their junior-high chatter. No one even hinted that I was mean or overbearing. And no one was angry about our near-catastrophy. Over dinner it struck me: the girls were elated—actually jubilant—over their own success at getting themselves out of a perilous situation and safely back to shore. Every girl had been afraid of capsizing, and every girl had made a decision to lean into the danger and pull! Like me, they had faced their fears and, with God's help, they had conquered them and had become victorious. *Breakthrough!* I breathed. *Thank you, God, for breakthrough!*

Sudden Loss

Chapter Ten

"Dear Linda," the letter began. I snuggled a little deeper into the quilts on my bed. I wanted to savor every word. "I am so glad you are able to come down to California. Mom and Dad want to take the family miniature golfing, and I have arranged to spend some time with the friends you enjoyed so much last time —and we will have several days to walk the trails while we talk about the plans for the wedding..."

I folded the cream-colored stationary and put it under my pillow and snapped out the light. In three days I would be driving with my friends to California to spend a week with my fiancé, and his family. My job with Trinity Western College allowed me the opportunity to step into the Public Relations department in the summertime doing student recruitment. This gave me the privilege of serving at the top Christian camps in California, and it was there where I met a certain young man. A year later we were engaged, and now the wedding was only three months away. Since I lived in Canada and he lived in the United States, we had corresponded by letters

Linda A. Olson

and phone calls. A long-distance relationship had not been easy, but we had managed to maintain what I thought was a healthy balance, and we developed what we had hoped would be the start of a long life together. When he proposed, I had not hesitated to accept. With many miles apart, I began making arrangements for a beautiful but modest church wedding. *Soon I will see him, see the sparkle in his warm brown eyes, feel his arms around me...* I drifted off to sleep.

*****

Life doesn't always go how we think it should. I had, of course, prayed about my upcoming marriage. But I had no idea that, an hour after my arrival, my fiancé would tell me he no longer had peace about our relationship and could not marry me. Thunderstuck, I could not believe my ears. We had talked, we had prayed....

What happened to the peace and joy you told me you had nine months ago when we were engaged? I screamed in my head.

My vision blurred; I could not look at him. He who had made me laugh, included me in his hopes and dreams, now could say nothing more than that he had no peace?

His Ways Are Higher

I turned from him, not bearing to look into his eyes. *Was there something he was keeping from me? Why didn't he say something before I made the twenty-three hour drive?*

His parents were nearly as grief-stricken as I; his father had just crafted our names into freshly-poured concrete, fully expecting to welcome me into the family. The loss I felt was not only for the young man, but also for his family whom I had grown to love. *How can I say good-bye to his mother and father, his brother, his sister? They were going to be my family, too. Lord, what happened?*

But I was met with silence. My pain-filled heart prayed my questions, and I sensed a dull, throbbing pain deep in my soul. I wanted so badly to hear a supernatural voice in my spirit telling me everything was going to be okay. Instead, the shock of the moment was eerily familiar—I could hardly believe what I had just heard.

And then I recognized it. Although the circumstances were completely different, the blow of sudden loss knocked the wind out of me, just like it had when I heard the news that Billy died.

No! I wanted to yell. *No! Not again! I loved you! You were supposed to be with me for always! Now, just like Billy, you've gone out of my life—and I have no idea why! Have I done something wrong?*

My head was spinning, my heart was broken. Again.

God was listening, God was silent. Again.

I couldn't bear to stay the rest of the week with the family I had hoped to call my own. I booked an early flight home. The friends that were to have celebrated with me at my bridal shower now drove me to the airport in communal silence, feeling my loss and not knowing what to say. My hopes and dreams for the future were shattered. What was there to say?

After parking the car at the terminal, my friend's husband grabbed my suitcase and the two of them flanked me as we walked through the double doors to the ticket counter. By special privilege they stayed with me until I was almost seated on the plane. Briefly we gave our last hugs, good-byes and shed more tears. They assured me they would come up to see me sometime.

The flight would give me time to think.

I had no idea how I would face my college family when the plane landed. They had sent me off with such good wishes, eager for me to return with excited plans for the wedding. Now the days ahead were uncertain, filled once more with many questions and few answers.

*****

His Ways Are Higher

"Allen, is this paperwork finished?" I held up the new forms we were introducing at the upcoming dorm meetings. My work had blessedly kept my hands busy and my thoughts diverted for the last several months. "If you don't need me anymore, I think I'll head for home. Edlyn and I are going out with Joan and Cathy to the Spaghetti House." Tonight, at the end of the week, I would relish light-hearted conversation served alongside some linguini.

"Looks like everything is good to go! Thanks, Linda. I appreciate all your hard work." Allen gave me a thumbs-up signal. "Have a great weekend!"

And I knew I would. With each passing day I had faced the "question of the day". First it was, *Will my parents think I will ever find a man?* Then it was, *How do I face the students with the news of my broken engagement?* Eventually it became, *What do I say when I have no answers myself?* And then I noticed that the questions came less and less frequently. The pursuit of answers seemed to be less and less important.

One morning I awoke with new resolve. *With God's help I made it through the loss of my baby brother; with God's help I will make it through a broken heart.*

No flashes of lightning.

No rolls of thunder.

Just the quiet assurance that He was with me. He had provided strength and courage for me in the past, and He would give me strength and healing now.

Finally, I had peace. His ways are higher.

Guilty as Charged

Chapter Eleven

"I don't think my parents have worked through their pain." I spoke quietly, but earnestly. Describing my parents was something I was fully prepared to do.

The counselor, a gentle lady in her mid-forties named Yvonne, sat opposite me. A student once more, I was working on a graduate degree in marriage and family counseling. The program required that I go through at least 25 hours of personal counseling and 25 hours of group counseling myself so that I would be better able to identify with future clients. I was eager to knock this requirement out quickly and focus on the other required classes in my program.

"Have you worked through *your* pain, Linda?" Her question was unexpected. Years had passed since Billy's death and I considered myself healthy, whole, and forward-moving.

"I believe I have." I responded with confidence, nodding my head.

When she had asked me to tell her about myself, I had willingly included a brief description of Billy's death before describing other areas of my life. Anyone who had a background like I had would know that time and a good prayer life heals most memories. And I seemed to be held in high esteem by my professors and classmates. I slept well at night and eagerly anticipated my future. I felt I was healthy and in no real need of professional help. I was just here to complete my college requirements.

"Yes," I repeated. "I believe I have."

Yvonne softly smiled, and I relaxed. Her comfortable office reflected her calm, easygoing manner, and the soft, dim light made it easy to talk. "We'll work on that when you are ready," she said.

Wait a minute. I turned my head slightly as if I hadn't heard correctly. I didn't need to work on anything. And I was certainly ready to get on with this assignment. What did she see that I was missing? Her statement left me baffled.

As I continued to see her each week, I grew to trust her with my most intimate feelings and thoughts. She was a good counselor, giving me insights into myself and helping me break through barriers in my life I never even knew existed. I realized I had several areas of my life that were benefiting from professional counseling.

His Ways Are Higher

Most people who heard about Billy's accident and my part in it immediately sympathized with me, then changed the subject. I could track the pattern with precision. Initially, they would express their condolences and then, in an unspoken way, I could sense they were glad the tragedy had not happened to them. Then came a brief silence while they wondered how I ever managed to get through that time in my life. And then they changed the subject.

Actually, I didn't really need to explain the situation further—my grief and questions had long ago melted into a conscious decision to set the whole thing aside in my heart. My tears had dried, my mind had matured, and I knew I would see Billy again someday. Case closed.

But that's not how it was, not really. The odd thing about counseling is that most of us want so badly to present to the world a healthy and put-together picture of ourselves that we pretend the picture is an accurate representation. We who might see a medical physician in a heartbeat if we discovered something amiss in our physical bodies nonetheless often refuse to address symptoms associated with emotional illness. We don't want to even turn in the direction that "something may be wrong" and we don't want to be seen as needy, as someone unable to cope independently. We don't relish the idea of telling a complete stranger our innermost feelings, risking possible abandonment even by a professional. Faithful friends are hard enough to come by; a one-way relationship with someone we pay to listen to us somehow goes against the grain of our self-reliance and privacy.

Still, some things we simply cannot figure out by ourselves. The mental and emotional energy we spend trying to solve our own problems drains our physical energy. Only after trying to solve the complex nature of some of our own questions—and coming up with less than adequate answers—are we willing to talk with someone and ask what they may see from a different perspective. The odd thing about professional counseling is that we are often afraid that something really *is* wrong with us, something that will label us crazy or weird. Yet we are caught by surprise when we discover that our inner pain has been caused by very real emotional splinters that have festered over time.

As helpful as Yvonne was in helping me solve some puzzles in my life, I still was eager to bring our sessions to a close. I had benefited greatly from her deep insights, and the immediate connection I had felt when we first met had broadened into a genuine, trusting professional relationship. I knew she cared, and I knew I could talk with her about anything.

One day I watched a movie of two brothers in a boating accident. One brother tried desperately to save the life of the other, but couldn't. His agony was reflected weeks later when he yelled at his psychologist, "This isn't fair!"

The psychologist, equally adamant, responded, "Whoever said life is fair?"

That brief exchange between two characters in a movie mirrored my own life exactly. I couldn't shake the parallel incident, and I couldn't get it out of my mind.

Although I felt I had dealt with my grief appropriately, I realized now that I had never addressed the accompanying guilt. I *was* guilty! I had killed my brother, however accidentally, and I had never been able to square that fact with myself.

At my next appointment, I shared my thoughts about the movie with Yvonne and she said, "You are ready, aren't you?" We both knew what she meant. I quietly nodded.

*****

"Tell me all about the accident, Linda," she said. "Start at the beginning, when you awakened that morning. Tell me everything—what you wore, what you expected was going to happen that day, and what really did happen. Go slowly, as if you were moving in slow motion. And along with describing what happened, tell me how you were feeling at every step of the way. Don't be afraid to cry if you feel the tears coming; you went through a tragic time, and tragic events necessitate sadness. I will be right here with you as you go through it in your memory." Her voice was soothing, assuring.

I folded my hands and refolded them. I nodded my head but found I couldn't speak. I crossed and uncrossed my legs, shifting in my seat. I really had no desire to open this door; somehow I knew that great pain was on the other side.

But Yvonne was looking at me, waiting. I looked down at my hands and felt my throat begin to tighten. I took a deep breath.

"I woke up before dawn. It was September 26th, and I had to get ready for school..."

Step by Step

Chapter Twelve

"It's okay, Linda, I'm right here."

Yvonne leaned forward. My quiet weeping broke into deep, heavy sobs.

I had killed Billy! I had killed my little brother who was the treasure of my heart. I didn't mean to—it had surely been an accident—but I nonethess had really killed him. I remembered his little-boy body so still in my arms….

My breath came in short gasps. Pain—incredible pain—surfaced in the counselor's office on that late summer day. I unconsciously held my sides, rocking back and forth like a baby. My chest heaved. I had walked into the terrible depths of realizing what had really happened: my brother had been crushed by the front end loader of the tractor as a result of my not being able to stop the tractor. The brakes never held. No sympathy from anyone could change that. No attempt at making me feel better could take away the truth: Billy died—he *died!*—because I couldn't stop the tractor.

Lord, take away the pain!

*****

Slowly I began to understand. I had confused grief with guilt. Easily, from the outside looking in, anyone could understand that Billy's death was an accident, and no one blamed me. We all lost Billy, and so we all grieved. Yet I had mistakenly thought that, because my family had forgiven me, all was well.

All was not well.

Grief, of course, is the painful expression of loss. And that expression takes many forms, some healthy and some not so healthy. But guilt is different. Guilt is the violating of a moral standard, and the knowledge of that violation is like holding a grenade. We instinctively know what we hold will eventually explode and hurt us if we hold it too long, but we have no idea how to get rid of it. Unless we are instructed somehow and sometime in the simple mechanics required to absolve the guilt, we have no idea if we will survive its explosive effects.

Acknowledging the cause of guilt is the first step. In my case, I had to admit that Billy died because of something I actually did. This I already knew, fundamentally. I even knew the second step: confession. I had not been afraid through the subsequent years to talk about the accident. I didn't speak cavalierly, but when an appropriate opportunity required the telling, I wasn't afraid to mention it.

Yet in my heart, I felt disconnected. Saying the words and confessing the action held different shades of meaning. Perhaps it was the intent of my heart—instead of the outside-looking-in kind of response—that required expression.

The third step was not altogether foreign to me either: asking forgiveness. In my growing relationship with Christ, I had taken care of this long ago, asking Him to forgive me of all my sin in general and for specific sins in particular. Naturally I had talked with my Best Friend and Savior about this most private of experiences and had asked Him to forgive me for what I had done to one of His beloved children.

But this step seemed to have more than one layer. After I had calmed somewhat from the initial surfacing of incredible pain that day, Yvonne led me to another room to gather my thoughts quietly. In those solitary moments, as I wiped the tears from my face, a question flashed through my mind.

"Have you forgiven yourself?"

I immediately recognized the voice of the Holy Spirit, and I marveled. In fifteen years I had never, ever addressed this matter; I had never thought to forgive *myself!* I knew God had forgiven me and I believed my parents had forgiven me, but how could I forgive myself?

And then that still, small voice said, *"Are you bigger than Me?"*

"No, God, I'm not bigger than You." I openly answered aloud.

"If you can trust Me to forgive you, do you not think I am big enough to help you forgive yourself?" The words came so clearly to my spirit.

I needed no other prompting. Right there in the small room next to the counseling office, I knelt by my chair. With God as my witness, I cried out, asking Him to help me forgive myself.

And He did. This had been the missing piece to the unrest in my soul.

Immediately I felt a huge burden lift. I experienced that deep peace that passed all my understanding. And a new freedom came.

I was amazed. I had been the one hindering my own growth! In thinking all was well, I had actually been making myself more emotionally ill. Now I knew I was standing on the firm footing modeled for me by Christ Himself. I was so grateful.

*****

"Dad?" I held the telephone receiver close to my ear, my hand trembling slightly. "Dad, are you there?" I began to cry even before I heard his voice.

A few weeks had passed since that eventful afternoon in Yvonne's office. Again I had gone to see the movie. Again I watched the scene with the boating accident. But this time my reaction had been completely different. This time I was calm and peaceful—caught up in the movie, to be sure—but not crushed by the identification with the characters. Since then, I had felt lighthearted and free. That was it—I was experiencing greater freedom in my life than ever before.

Only one question remained; only one more layer of the third step of forgiveness, and it was framed in a question: *Has Dad forgiven me?*

I already knew no one in my family blamed me for the accident with Billy; their love for me had remained constant and unchanging.Yet when I had pursued the question with Yvonne, she simply asked me to call my father.

Call Dad?

The thought struck me as completely foreign. Dad was not someone with whom I discussed personal matters. Deep down, I really did feel he had forgiven me, but I had no idea that pain still existed in his own heart. I had killed not only my little brother, but my father's youngest son. I felt I was facing, even mentally, the very real possibility that Dad would reject me outright if I spoke openly about the issue.

Better let sleeping dogs lie, I reasoned. *It has been over fifteen years now and we have gotten along fine; no need to rock the boat.*

Still, my conscience would not let me rest. My heart pounded every time I thought about calling him. Could I really do it?

Finally, I answered my own question. *If I don't even ask, then I may never know the answer.* That settled it. Asking God to give me the courage, I picked up the receiver and, after wiping my eyes, dialed the familiar number.

One ring. Two rings. Three rings...

I held my breath. *Perhaps he's visiting the neighbors. Or maybe he's napping; I'll call back later.* But before I could remove the receiver from my ear, I heard the phone stop mid-ring.

"Hello?" His voice was deep, familiar.

I couldn't talk. The tears, silent at first, now poured from my eyes as I openly sobbed.

"Hello?" he said again. "Hello?"

Finally, I spoke. "Dad, it's Linda." More tears. And then, without saying anything else, I blurted out my question. "Dad, have you forgiven me for little Billy?"

I held my free hand to my mouth, forcing myself to hold my breath so I could hear his answer. *Oh, please,* I prayed. *Please let him say yes.* I stopped sobbing and forced myself to listen. Was he never going to speak?

And then I heard it. Dad was crying too. In a moment, in that same deep voice, came the confident reply.

"...a long time ago."

I let out my breath in a rush. Dad had forgiven me! He forgave me long ago! I was ecstatic. Quickly I wiped my face of the tears that had been flowing down my cheeks.

And then, much to my surprise, another question surfaced, one I had wanted to ask for years but had felt was too forward for a daughter to ask her father, a man from a generation that didn't talk openly of such things. Still, he had responded affirmatively to my first inquiry. Maybe he would answer just one more? I took a breath.

"Dad, do you love me?"

He blew his nose. I could picture him pulling out the red handkerchief he always kept in the back pocket of his overalls. A moment passed, then another. He sniffed. "Why shouldn't I?"

My upside-down world suddenly turned right-side up! *Oh, how wonderful!* I felt a warm rush go through me. *My father loved me!*.

"I just needed to hear you say that." I smiled into the phone, cradling the receiver, pressing it into my ear so the words would be closer to my heart.

Finally, it was enough.

A Tough Go

Chapter Thirteen

"Linda Ann Bergen."

My name, spoken by the President of Biola University, blared from the loudspeaker to several thousand people gathered in the outdoor courtyard of the school I had been attending for graduate studies.

I took a deep breath, and stepped forward—stepped forward to grasp the hand of the Dean and to take hold of my hard-earned diploma. Stepped forward into a new future filled with whatever God had in store for me. The gold tassel swayed on my black mortarboard. My smile could not have been bigger.

I turned from the photographer and scanned the crowd. There, in her best Sunday dress and shoes and with her head held high, sat Mom with my two sisters and a family friend. Mom caught my eye, nodded, and then began clapping wildly with the others. I smiled back, my eyes misting.

Does life get any better?

"Linda Ann Bergen." Once again the loudspeaker broadcast my name. It was no mistake. I rose and proudly walked down the aisle again to receive a *second* diploma, a symbol of God's gracious strength in me. My classmates stood to their feet, surprising me as they shouted at the top of their lungs. They were not about to miss this moment of celebrating with me.

*****

It had been a tough go. I loved learning, and college life proved to be a fulfilling challenge. Yet I was impatient to conclude this educational trail; the constant pressure to complete my studies with excellence was wearing on me. Counseling the students at the college where I worked had been a joy, and I knew I could make counseling a satisfying career. Then I discovered that professional counseling required a Master's degree, and my heart sank.

Do I have it in me to pursue another two years of higher education?

I had looked hard into my heart, re-examining my motives. Added to my anxiety was the knowledge that my Bible School credits may not be accepted at the graduate level, and so discouragement flooded in. *What now?*

His Ways Are Higher

By God's providence I was introduced to Dr. Norman Wright, the director of a Marriage and Family Counseling program at a Southern California university. The program had high requirements, and only fifteen students would be accepted. Norm Wright encouraged me to apply—and I did—only to receive a rejection letter indicating I had not met the standards. I continued to attend classes, took my Graduate Record exam and two years later met with Norm again.

He encouraged me to continue my pursuit. "You are just the kind of student we are looking for," he said.

I took his advice, only to receive another rejection letter. A few more years passed, and I pursued bringing up my grade point average as well as retaking the Graduate Record exam for the third time. Unfortunately the test scores dropped and my GPA did not meet the school standards so I was rejected a third time.

Now, wait a minute, God, I fumed. *It's been five years. Just what is it you are trying to tell me?*

This is the hard part in walking by faith: sometimes His leading just can't be tracked. In the undertaking of my education, I thought I was following God's guidance, only to have the doors closed and, apparently, locked. What did He want me to do? He had led me this far, I was sure, but now what did He have in store for me?

Linda A. Olson

I knew God was not a Divine Deity who only sits in heaven and watches the world go 'round. He had shown Himself to me clearly the last several years, and I knew He loved me, had forgiven me, had led me this far, and had taken the entire incident with Billy—something that could have derailed me for life—and turned it into a springboard to knowing Him intimately. I knew He actively cared about me.

I also knew I had some decisions to make. I prayed, asking simply that He would lead me.

And I waited.

His answer was not long in coming. I had been applying to the university, but I soon discovered that on the same campus was a seminary which offered a Master's Degree in Christian Education with an emphasis in Counseling. I decided to apply there and, to my great surprise, was accepted immediately. I could complete the degree in a year and two summers. I shook my head in amazement. Who but God could have worked out this plan?

My walk with the Lord was deepening; what I had thought would be a second-best choice seemed to be the first choice with God.

A week after I started my summer studies at Talbot Seminary, Norm Wright approached me. "*I am no longer head of the Marriage and Family counseling program, Linda, but I would like you to meet with Dr.*

Hulgus, the director and tell her you want to get into the program," he said.

I was completely taken aback. *Why was this coming up again?* I had completely let go of the possibility of entering this particular program. Yet, once again I followed Norm's counsel and met with Dr. Hulgus. She carefully explained that, besides working hard in the program, I would be required to pick up two pre-requisites in the summer and earn at least a C grade. If I would do that, I would be accepted on probation into the very program I had originally wanted and been rejected from three times. Hard work didn't scare me (after all, if there was one thing Dad had taught me on the farm, it was hard work), and so I walked out of the office after agreeing to the proposed plan and attempted to catch my breath.

Is God moving on my behalf to do what I thought was impossible? I blinked back sudden tears.

I checked schools in Canada as well as in California to see who was offering the two required summer classes and to my amazement there was only one school available, twenty minutes from where I lived. I took the two three-week crash courses and earned a C in each class. I was in! I could hardly believe it!

Soon I was immersed in my studies and, with plans to return to Canada upon graduation, I planned to make the most of my two years in Southern California. All seemed to be going along well until halfway through the plan. Because the Marriage and Family counseling program seemed to overlap with another psychology program, Biola decided to dissolve the Marriage & Family counseling program. Although we were told they would help us get the required classes, it didn't seem to be happening. Then, much to my surprise, I was called into the registrar's office only to be told that someone had made the mistake of sending in my two-year student visa to the immigration office and now it had been returned, indicating I had to be completed with school in one and a half years. Then, after starting work at a large church, the administrator informed me that they could not pay me because I was Canadian!

If after five years God had so clearly confirmed this next step in my career, then why was all this happening? Had I not experienced enough loss? I found myself grieving again, and then I realized that the stages of grief (first described in Elizabeth Kubler-Ross' *On Death and Dying)* not only apply to an actual death but to any major loss. (The stages include denial, anger, bargaining, depression, and finally acceptance.) When I finally moved past my resistance to go to graduate school, I felt I had to let go of this dream, too.

It seemed everything was going wrong. No money, no opportunity to work, no help with my classes and my student visa was shortened. Fighting back the tears, I made an appointment with the President of the college. I became fond of the saying,"When the going gets tough, the tough get going."

I shared my dilemma with the President. He told me what I was not prepared to hear. "The things you are learning now will prepare you for your career field much more than anything we could teach you in the classroom." I wasn't sure if I should be comforted or not.

That was it. The appointment was over. He ushered me into an adjoining room to meet with the Vice-President. Soon the phone rang.

A professor from the other program offered to assist me with any additional classes I needed.

The church set up an appointment and covered my fees to meet with an immigration attorney.

Someone told me that Biola had Canadian scholarships available. It wouldn't be much, but it would certainly help.

The college Sunday-school teacher I assisted handed me his credit card and said, "Go fill your car with gas."

Another Sunday-school class took a love-offering to help with my groceries.

I was interning at Norman Wright's office and one of my fellow interns handed me a check, saying, "It's not much, but my wife and I wanted to give you something." The check was made out for the exact amount I needed to pay rent that day.

With God's grace surrounding me at every turn, I went through that summer with every need met. I rejoiced continually.

*****

Then the it-doesn't-make-any-sense stuff started happening again.

In November, the immigration attorney called. "I have good news and bad news. The good news is that your student visa has been extended another semester and you have a part-time work visa. The bad news is you have to be a full time student."

I was dumbfounded. I had only one more class to take, so I could not qualify as a full-time student. Three weeks before Christmas I didn't know if I was moving back to Canada or just going up for Christmas.

And then once again, God showed up.

For the first time ever, Talbot Seminary offered the exact classes I needed to complete a second Master's. With both my undergraduate classes in Christian Education and the graduate classes I had just taken, I would qualify to complete a double Master's with only one more semester.

His Ways Are Higher

As humbling as it was for me to ask my Dad if I could borrow money for my last semester of school (since I had paid cash for all my education), he was in a position to help and was honored that I asked.

Isaiah 40:31 became a favorite verse: "But those who wait on the LORD shall renew their strength; They shall mount up with wings like eagles; They shall run and not be weary, They shall walk and not faint."

Finally, I came to my last semester at Biola University. My heart was filled with deep joy and gratitude. God had shown Himself faithful repeatedly, and I was delighting in a season of simple but abundant blessing. I received a contract in the mail, offering me my former job as Dean of Women at Trinity Western College, and I immediately signed on the dotted line, peace

welling up in my heart. Now, here I was, with a double degree in hand, a job awaiting me back home, and a family who loved me. Perhaps life was straightening out, after all. In fact I began to think, *Can life get any better?*

"I Just Knew"

Chapter Fourteen

"Take me out to the ballgame; take me out with the crowd…" I swayed with the singing fans, quickly learning the words to the famous American song. I was in the stands of a baseball stadium where the Angels were playing a pre-season game, and I was having the time of my life. I wiped the mustard from my fingers, the hot dog having been consumed just a few moments before. Rick, a handsome new friend, had invited me to join him and his family at a baseball game in Palm Springs, and we were having a wonderful time.

As Rick drove me home after the game, I mentioned that I had just signed a contract that week and so I would be leaving for Canada in two months. When he said good-bye that night, I didn't know if I would ever see him again.

But the next week, the phone rang and Rick offered me three different dates. I was so excited I said without a moment's hesitation, "I'll take them!"

Linda A. Olson

It didn't take long before we knew we wanted to share life together. I smiled as I remembered someone once saying to me, "When you meet the right guy, you will just know."

When I met Rick, I just knew.

Does life get any better? Yes, it does. Standing next to me on graduation day was my fiancé.

*****

Rick looked at me carefully, his hands holding mine. I had just told him about the accident with Billy.

"You must have felt terrible, Linda," he said. "How did you ever get through those next several years?" His eyes spoke from such a tender heart.

I had thought that he must know my background before we were married. He had shown his love for me in countless ways, yet I wanted him to be absolutely sure he knew me thoroughly.

Knew what he was getting into, I thought wryly. After all, I myself wondered how I would handle marriage and motherhood. Would I panic in emergency situations? Be overprotective with children of our own, knowing what had happened to my little brother when he was just two-and-a-half?

His Ways Are Higher

I thought I had made great strides in working through the grief and guilt over Billy's accident, but common sense told me they could surface again in my own future family.

"Honey," Rick began again. "I can't imagine the pain you've gone through. Your family must have been devastated! And you all never talked about it? It's amazing you even have relationships with each other; the death of a child produces the worst emotional pain possible."

Rick still held my hands. "Parents often split up, siblings blame each other; either the family deals with it or they don't. If they don't, relationships are rarely more than perfunctory and superficial."

I lifted my eyes. *Who was the counselor in this relationship anyway?* I smiled. Rick was right on target, and I knew it. His compassion brought fresh tears as I realized that he would never judge me for Billy's death, never bring it up in any future argument, never distrust me with our own children someday. My heart overflowed with love for him. *Where did you come from?* I thought. *I don't know and I don't care; I'm just never going to let you go!*

In a few months, we would be husband and wife.

*****

Rick was a real gem. He patiently listened as I poured out every detail of my journey since the accident, and he only assured me more of his love. With confidence that, should anything ever come up related to Billy's death, I would move through it with Rick's support, we began making plans for a late July wedding in Manitoba, Canada, where my parents lived. We would then move to British Columbia so that I could fulfill my contract obligations. However, when my supervisor at Trinity heard of our upcoming marriage, he called to ask me to reconsider our arrangement. He was uncomfortable with my working fulltime when I would be a newlywed. Although I agreed to pray about the matter, seeking counsel during that time and eventually becoming even more convinced of my decision, the offer to work at Trinity Western was withdrawn. What complicated matters even further was that someone was hired to take Rick's position as school administrator exactly the same day.

I was dumbstruck again. *Had I heard from God clearly?* The whole arrangement had seemed hand-in-glove as Rick had been offered work in the Public Relations department at the same college. Now, here we were, a few weeks before the wedding and we were both unemployed!

Once again life wasn't making any sense. But this time I was getting the hang of going to my Heavenly

Father first, checking my heart for anything that might be amiss, and listening carefully for any direction from the One who loved me most.

I determined that this time, I wouldn't be derailed.

And I wasn't for I knew His ways are higher!

"I Do"

Chapter Fifteen

"You know, Linda, we may never have this opportunity again. We have no commitments to jobs, we may not have much money," Rick said, "but I'll do anything for work. We have our entire future ahead of us. Let's go ahead with our original plans to visit with your family, get married in Canada, and go on our honeymoon before we head back home to the States." Rick made it sound so wonderful. It didn't make a bit of sense, but it sounded great.

I considered what he said. "Well, I really was looking forward to having you meet my extended family and experience a little of how I grew up," I told him. I inwardly prayed for guidance. "I don't sense the Lord directing otherwise, so…I agree!" I threw my arms around his neck.

Truly, this is how I wanted to live my life.

*****

My mother in Manitoba was taking care of some of the wedding plans, and I did what I could from the States. Soon all arrangements had been made, giving me two full weeks to introduce Rick to the small community where I grew up. He met my large extended Mennonite family and enjoyed fresh vegetables from the garden and delicious homemade pies every night. In the evenings after dinner, we took long walks, talking about our coming days while we fought off the mosquitoes.

The wedding was simple, and the joy was abundant. I couldn't have been happier as I approached my handsome bridegroom, waiting for me at the front of the church.

After the ceremony we drove down Main Street honking the horn on our car. We saw only one person in the entire neighborhood, and he was jogging. Rick asked, "Where is everyone?"

I laughed. "They're at the campground waiting for us!"

The dining room at the campground was the only place we could find that was big enough for our celebration. In a small community nearly everyone comes to a celebration. I'm not sure if they came to witness the wedding or if they just wanted to celebrate with us. But it didn't matter—all were welcome and we were eager to share our joy. And did we ever celebrate! Our hearts were bursting with God's abundant blessings: joy, peace, laughter, friends, family, food...the list went on and on.

After the reception we flew from Winnipeg, Canada, and honeymooned in the beautiful area of Banff, Alberta, in the Rocky Mountains. After several days, we made our way to British Columbia where I had once worked. We welcomed former friends to an Open House and then we gathered my belongings and headed to Palmdale, California, to make our home. I drove with Dr. Thompson, one of our faculty members, who had spoken to the border guards the night before and who had assured us everything would be fine. Rick proceeded ahead, then pulled to the side of the road and waited.

*****

That night the border guards changed crossings.

Now we were dealing with strangers who had no compassion whatsoever. After ushering Dr. Thompson and I inside for further questioning, the border guard challenged me.

"Why didn't you turn this in?" He held up my student visa.

I was bewildered; I had worked with an immigration attorney to have all the necessary paperwork completed in advance of the border crossing. The guard waited for my answer.

"I wasn't aware I needed to do that." I spoke honestly, respectfully.

The blue-uniformed guard looked at me as if he didn't believe me. He waved my visa again. "It says right here on the back of your visa; it's written in Spanish."

My eyes widened, but I said nothing. The guard was studying me, waiting for my response. I felt I was being baited for a confrontation and I decided on the spot not to take the bait. I remained silent.

The guard spoke again, his voice irritated. "I'll bet you don't understand Spanish?"

Now I spoke—quietly, purposely controlling my breathing and the tone of my voice. "That's right," I said. Silently I prayed for wisdom and protection.

The guard raised his voice. "Where is your marriage license?"

My heart sank. Dr. Thompson and I exchanged glances. The license was with Rick's father who had married us. Rick's parents would be traveling for another two weeks before we could contact them. I confidently but quietly explained the situation.. "What else could I have done?" I asked respectfully.

The guard thundered at us. "You could have married in the United States! Just get your marriage license and come back."

My jaw dropped. This was a 1500-mile trip, not a jaunt down the road. We stood silently, wondering what to do next. The security guard motioned to another guard to check our vehicle.

His partner responded, "Are you going to let them go?"

I wanted badly to turn my head to see the response, but I didn't dare. Their conversation continued and we sensed that the second guard shared our faith in Christ and also Dr. Thompson's passion for Political Science.

This guard walked with us to our car, opened the back, and said quietly, "We'll just talk a few minutes to make it appear like I am checking your things." He straightened up and said, a bit loudly, "You're welcome to go."

Forty-five minutes later, with grateful hearts, Rick and I were united again.

Troubles, Tests, and Termination

Chapter Sixteen

The board member spread his toast with some jam. "We need to talk about your probation."

We had met for breakfast to talk about my work as the new Program Director and Counselor at our local domestic violence shelter. Being newly married, I was pleased to find Monday-through-Friday work to coincide with Rick's schedule. The daily eight-hour shift would go toward the three thousand supervised hours that were required for my Marriage and Family Therapy license.

Two months into my employment, the director of the shelter asked me to step into her position because she would be leaving. Although the work would have been fulfilling, I also knew the job carried more responsibility than I wanted at this time, especially since I was a newlywed. I respectfully declined the offer and continued with my duties.

Now the board member was talking about probation.

I spoke with surprise. "I am happy to talk about that, but what 'probation' are you referring to?" I had been put on the payroll immediately and, as far as I knew, I had been meeting their expectations in my position.

The board member raised his eyebrows and gulped the last of his coffee. "Didn't the director tell you that you were on probation?"

'No," I said. "This is the first I have heard of it."

"Well, just forget it." He hurriedly drew out his wallet to pay for breakfast.

I was bewildered. I didn't know what was going on. *What was this talk about probation?*

Soon I discovered that the director's plan in hiring me was that I would be in place to take over her job when she left. When I declined her offer, she changed my employment status to probationary without telling me. Over the next few months, I heard nothing more, so I thought all was resolved.

Another director was hired, and we often clashed. Our counseling styles differed significantly, and she often scheduled me to counsel women who had made decisions for Christ earlier in their lives. These women had not become strong in their faith, however, and so they had made poor choices. I wasn't sure if I was being assigned these clients because I was familiar with spiritual struggles or if the director simply wanted me to handle more complex cases.

One day she called me into her office and spoke harshly. "I have drawn up a job description and am putting you on two-month's probation to see if you meet the requirements for the job, effective immediately."

I was astonished. "I have worked here for nearly a year, and just now I am getting a job description? This feels more like a threat than a job description." I struggled to control the astonishment in my voice. The director offered no further explanation, and I knew the brief meeting was over.

Although I didn't understand the reason for the probation, I nevertheless faithfully checked my list almost daily to be sure I was meeting all requirements. Several weeks later I was scheduled to be "on call" in the case of an emergency. I was coming into town when I was delayed because of a flat tire. The next morning the director called me into her office.

"I have never done this before, but I am firing you," she said with a sharp tone. She wouldn't even look at me.

Once again I was dumbfounded. *Did I just hear her correctly?*

I sat quietly and, after a few moments, responded respectfully. "What could I have done to meet your expectations?"

She looked up, her eyes dark, her voice flat. "There isn't anything you could have done."

Once again I felt unjustly treated.

Betrayal is never easy. I felt that all my time as Program Director and Counselor had been of no value, that the quality of my work had been disregarded, and that the whole situation reeked of unfairness. Life is like that sometimes. Nothing about this situation made sense to me, and now I would need to start all over again to look for a job to meet the requirements for my license. Had all my time at the shelter been wasted?

Here was another situation that seemed to have more questions than answers. Personally I was offended at the callous attitude the management of the shelter had displayed to me, and I was surprised that they would not honor their contractual agreement, especially since I was meeting the requirements for the job.

Still, terminating my employment was their decision, and their words and actions stung. They didn't want me there and I didn't know what I had done that warranted the terminatioin of my employment.

In the following months, I talked the whole situation over with Rick, prayed about a proper response, and eventually challenged the board on their decision, all to no avail. Once again, I faced the question of what to do about a situation that seemed to be final, only this time the question was intensely personal. *What was I to do with the deep hurt in my heart?*

Sometimes it comes down to that—a time when you have done all you know to do and the situation still doesn't pan out. When Billy was hurt, the doctor did everything he knew to do, and Billy still died. I prayed as hard as I could, and he still died. And every single person who knew Billy also knew that he had died as a result of my actions. Every single person, to some degree, faced that growing hurt in his own heart, a hurt that could have been directed at me. Yet, over the months and years, no one came to me in bitterness. Always, I was approached with compassion and care, a silent forgiveness evidenced by words and actions.

Now it was my turn: would I harbor resentment over the unfairness of my job loss, or would I forgive the people who hurt me for no justifiable reason?

I considered carefully. Making a decision to "keep my side of the sidewalk clean" required an inner heart-search, an action I did not take lightly. Knowing that *not* forgiving the director and the board members would only fuel the embers of my anger, I chose to forgive. After all, I reasoned, Christ had long ago forgiven me.

Closing my eyes, I spoke quietly to the Lord. "Father, what they did wasn't right. Neither was it right what people did to You. I forgive them. Please help me get past my hurt".

In forgiving the people who had hurt me, I realized that my employment was terminated not because of any inner weakness, but possibly because of my inner strength.

Something—I didn't know what—had challenged the people at the shelter; perhaps they didn't know what to do with that.

But now I knew I could face the future. I was able to step forward with new strength knowing God's hand of protection was upon me.

*****

Forgiving was not easy; I cared deeply for the abused women who came to me for counsel at the shelter. Many were young and frightened. Some decided the only answer to violence was to flee the abuser instead of attempting reconciliation. One woman embraced my support and, with leaning on the Lord, developed the courage and strength to set firm boundaries, standing up to the man who had hurt her. This assertive action changed her life as she recognized she was worthy of respect. I asked God one specific question: *Why would You take me out of this position when these women need so much encouragement?*

The question was later compounded when I requested the signature of my supervising board member to sign off on a year's worth of counseling hours towards my state license, and she refused to provide it. Although by that time my heart had healed, I also stood firm, telling her I would report her to the state board if she continued to refuse. I wondered if she would ever give me a favorable reference for future employment. I waited for her response.

Reluctantly, she signed off on my hours and, as it turned out, my next employer never asked where I had worked previously.

God had gone ahead of me again and opened doors of favor.

Conscience Clear

Chapter Seventeen

The doctor's tone was calm and professional. "I'm concerned. She isn't gaining weight like she should be." We guessed that "concerned" carried a more serious definition at the moment.

Our precious Melinda Ann—her name means "beautiful and gracious one"—had entered our world nearly five weeks before her due date, weighing only five pounds, eleven ounces. Now, at seventeen months, she weighed only seventeen pounds, and her appetite was dwindling. What little food she took in came right back up. Although Rick and I had been experiencing God's peace for several years as husband and wife, parenting introduced an entirely new dimension. We were jolted out of our reverie by the doctor's next words. "I am referring her to Children's Hospital in Los Angeles; the situation requires a specialist."

Immediately I felt anxiety rise. I told myself to calm down; anxiety was normal at a time like this. But I also felt a sharp panic in my spirit. My heart cried out in prayer again. *God! We have dedicated our baby to You—and she is yours—but something is wrong!* My mind raced to find a path of understanding, a reason for our daughter's ill health. *Why would You allow such a beautiful innocent baby to stop growing?* I could sense an accusing tone, even in my silent prayer. This was God's doing.

And then, unexpectedly, guilt surfaced. I had done something dreadfully wrong several years ago with Billy, hadn't I? And the child's breath had ceased. Had I done something wrong now? Was history repeating itself? Desperately I searched my heart. *God, please show me if there is something else I can do. Please!*

*****

And so it goes. In a world of cause and effect, we naturally look to a cause when we see a devastating effect. If we have been burned, perhaps we have touched a hot pot. Remembering childhood experiences when we were taught right from wrong by immediate consequence, we may confuse discipline with natural brokenness. We may grow into adulthood by reversing that reasoning: we see a consequence and search for the cause. If we are in pain, we suspect we have done something wrong. This natural reaction may indeed be true at times (we may gain weight if we overeat), but not always.

Wisdom requires we first ask ourselves if we have had any part—intentional or unintentional—in a situation.

In parenting especially, we have so much to learn! Yet many times our hearts come up clean; accidents happen and babies get sick. They just do. And we have no direct contribution in causing them.

This is where bewilderment can settle in. We know that God wants desperately for us to know He loves us. We think, *If He loves me, He wouldn't cause me pain*.

Therefore, when we *are* in pain, He must not love us. It may not be true, but that is our rationale. We seem to take the "if-then" approach to life. Throw in previous trauma, and our spiritual reasoning goes askew. In the moment of panic, we simply want God to "fix it—quick!"

And He can. We do not deny the incredible, powerful healing hand of the Almighty. Yet God does all in His power to blanket us with Himself, to let us know He is present *with* us in our troubles and in our day-to-day lives. Often we do not witness immediate physical healing, and we naturally ask if we are somehow hindering that movement of God.

However, the enemy—satan himself—opposes life and all that goes with it. He specializes in fanning the embers of unknown panic into the flames of tormenting confusion and fear. This is where honest questioning comes in, asking God to reveal truth and knowledge.

*****

We sat in the office of Dr. Emard, a local chiropractor. The doctors at Children's Hospital had checked Melinda and found no cause for her declining health, yet her weight was much less than normal and she could not keep any food down.

As life would have it, in the midst of concern for our daughter, I was in a car accident. My car had been rear-ended so hard that I landed in a ditch across the road, facing the opposite direction. I suffered a medium whiplash, but was profoundly grateful I was not more seriously injured. In the aftermath of the accident, several friends had recommended Dr. Emard and his chiropractic care to help with my recovery.

In the ensuing appointments, I mentioned Melinda's condition. He listened carefully and, as he already had been seeing young children in his practice, invited me to bring her in for a brief assessment.

So here we were, little two-year-old Melinda—all of twenty pounds—sitting timidly on my lap, pale and listless. Dr. Emard tenderly rubbed her head and checked her spine. He looked at me and grinned. "Be ready—she'll be very hungry by the time you get home."

I blinked. How could that be? He had done nothing—absolutely nothing. I almost laughed out loud. Rick and I had tried every trick in the book to get our "beautiful and gracious one" to eat even the corner of a piece of toast. Nevertheless, I stood, thanked Dr. Emard politely for his time, and walked dumbfounded back to our car. I wondered as I buckled Melinda into her car seat. *Did he really know what he was saying?*

*****

As soon as we arrived home, Rick greeted us and I told him of our appointment with the chiropractor. While I put Melinda into her high chair and tied a bib around her neck, I voiced my frustration that I had subjected our daughter to yet another doctor who didn't know what was wrong. In a few minutes I set before Melinda a late breakfast of toast, juice, and a scrambled egg. Rick and I sat at the table too, sipping some tea, talking quietly. In a moment, we both put our cups down. Melinda was eating! In no time flat, our little girl gobbled the food on her plate and was soon asking for more. We were astonished! Rick asked me to explain to him again what in the world the chiropractor had done.

"He just rubbed her head and checked her spine!" I watched Melinda, my mouth agape. I didn't understand how rubbing her head and checking her spine could possibly affect her appetite, but I didn't care that I didn't understand. Our baby was eating!

On our next visit to the chiropractor, Dr. Emard explained to me that Melinda had had a pinched nerve in her neck that repressed the "appetite" messages to her brain, so she simply hadn't felt the need to eat. When he had rubbed her head to stimulate the pituitary gland and checked her spine, he had gently adjusted the spinal column to alleviate the pinched nerve, and so now the appetite messages were coming through.

Immediately Melinda started on a growth spurt and became full of energy. Although we were now on our toes racing after an active toddler, we were glad to be doing it. And we became even more ardent believers in the practice of chiropractic.

As I thought about the entire experience, I realized that God had granted our request for a healthy daughter at birth. Now, in a time of trial, He had positioned us where our faith had to be stretched in a much larger way. Would we still trust Him in the face of a medical storm? Although I had questioned myself deeply, truth won out, and God had led us to someone with greater knowledge of our daughter's condition.

I had forgiven myself long ago of the part I had played in Billy's death. And I had rightly questioned myself to see if I had any part in Melinda's condition. But my search had come up with nothing; my conscience was clear. So now I had found my guilt to be unfounded.

God had taught me something more about life.

Forgiveness Times Two

Chapter Eighteen

I looked at our newly-born second daughter, hooked up to all kinds of monitors in an infant incubator, and turned to the doctor. "Is she going to be okay?"

Our beautiful Karine Dawn—her name means "purity and rising"—had made her debut appropriately in the wee hours of Easter morning. The delivery had gone well and the baby had weighed nearly eight pounds, so I was puzzled when the pediatric nurse brought newborns to the other mother in my room but silently walked past me. Fighting an increasing inner fear, I crawled out of bed and made my way to the infant nursery where our little baby lay under bright lights, her eyes swathed in bandages.

The doctor looked at me, quick to smile her reassurance. "Yes, your baby will be fine; we're simply checking her vitals. She has a good case of jaundice and must be watched closely, but you may take her home tomorrow. A nurse will come to your house regularly to check her bilirubin levels." She scribbled her signature on the hospital release form.

Rick and I were incredibly relieved to take our baby girl home with us the next day. And Melinda, at nineteen months, loved to bring a little book to Karine in her little incubator, and sit close, pretending to read to her little sister.

*****

Karine was only three years old when we noticed a small mole on her knee. Eventually the mole grew to the size of a pencil eraser. Doctors assured us that it seemed to be harmless, but they would remove it if we insisted. We insisted. The simple out-patient procedure exploded into an all-out fight with Karine when she panicked at the sight of the needle in the nurse's hand. Her screams could be heard throughout the doctor's office, and Rick tried to hold her down as she tried to bolt from the examining table. Karine stared at me, wild-eyed, as if I had tricked her. Nurses on either side of her grabbed a flailing arm, Rick held her feet so she could not kick, and the doctor put on his gloves.

Her voice pierced the air again as her eyes locked on mine. "Mom, why do you let them do this to me?"

Her screams echoed the cries of my heart. As Karine cried out to me, I now cried out to the Lord.

God, where are you in this? My little girl thinks I am the one causing her pain!

I held Karine's shoulders tightly; she was wrapped in a little papoose, exposing only her knee for the procedure. Medication had done nothing to relax our three-year-old. I bent my head, weeping silently. I was helpless to convince Karine that this was for her good. And I wondered.

Would she ever forgive me?

*****

And isn't it just so? We see a situation so plainly when we are the caring parent and our child is the one who hurts. Yet it is something else again when we are in the child's place and we make no sense of our Father's plan. He who can see all, from beginning to end, wants us to trust Him in the midst of situations we do not understand, in the times when we cannot possibly know the bigger picture.

We, of course, knew more than Karine. In order to find out if the mole was cancerous, the mole had to be removed. To "let it be" would be to put Karine's health in jeopardy. But how was I to handle life when I was the one who was in pain? When I couldn't make sense out of what was happening? When I felt betrayed by God?

God does not want us to hurt any more than we wanted Karine to hurt. His motives are good, as ours were for our daughter. And He loves us. Although we had loved Karine for three years—caring for her and doing all that parents ought to do—when it came right down to it, she didn't trust us because she was in pain. Surely we did not want her to be in pain, but we knew that treatment was imperative as a mole can become cancerous, and cancer can include increasing degrees of pain. For *her* good, we allowed—gave permission for and even aided in—a procedure that caused her pain.

But Karine could not see the big picture; she could not understand what must be done today in order for good health tomorrow. All I could hope for was that I had built enough trust in her, day by day, so that she would trust me with the unknown. In her own pain, she could not see that her anguish and subsequent accusation of me pierced my own heart.

Is this what had happened with Billy? I wondered.

The pain of his death had sliced through me, and I had asked God if that excruciating heartache would ever go away. I also had asked Him how anything good could possibly come out of such intense pain. Why would He allow such an accident to happen? Didn't he care about Billy? Didn't he care about us? Didn't He care about *me*? Our hearts had been broken, and I had often wondered if mine would *ever* mend. Now, years later, witnessing Karine's inner fear turned outward into screams of terror, I could only silently weep. In my own pain, had I carried a distrust of God into my adulthood?

Did I need, in my own way, to forgive God for allowing Billy's death?

I thought some more. Perhaps forgiveness was not the best word to describe the melting in my soul. God knew all; He had fashioned me from before my birth. He had placed me in a family that included a lively little boy, and He had now brought me a husband and our own young children.

I bowed my head, still hearing Karine's screams. I wanted to trust Him; I really did. I knew God was taking care of Billy in heaven just as we were doing all we knew to take care of our daughter on earth. I was in the exact position Karine was in.

Would I trust the one who loved me?

*****

Karine was still kicking and arching her back. My vision blurred with tears. I closed my eyes and made my decision. I would trust Him. I came to Him silently but directly. *God, where are you in this? Please help!* The doctor performed the procedure as quickly as he could, even with a splitting headache brought on by our screaming child.

A kind receptionist opened the door and poked her head into the room. "Karine, would you like to hold a balloon? And I have a coupon here for some frozen yogurt if your mommy and daddy would like to take you out after the procedure."

Immediately, Karine relaxed and her smile returned. My cry for heavenly help had been answered almost immediately.

Three weeks later we received a call with the news that the mole on Karine's knee had indeed been pre-cancerous. Another surgery would be required to be sure they had gotten it all. Rick and I looked at each other, concern in our eyes. We didn't relish the idea of an exhausting repeat performance with Karine in the doctor's office.

As expected, Karine did not take kindly to another procedure. Her screams were again heard by everyone in the office. We felt the now-familiar parental tension between doing what we believed to be best for our daughter and her own personal pain. In the months that followed we became even more grateful that God had guided us to insist on the first surgery and that He had protected us from what could have been much worse circumstances. Karine had no further complications.

Until five years later.

*****

Karine was eight years old when Rick, wrestling with her on the floor, grabbed her right arm and felt a significant growth just above her wrist. Once again, we acted immediately and, within a week, surgery was scheduled.

I was quite concerned about Karine's reactions to doctors by now. As I prayed for God to protect her once again and to help her with the upcoming procedure, I made a conscious effort to stem my own apprehension about accompanying a screaming child through necessary surgery.

A few days before the appointment, Karine came to me as I was painting windowsills in our bedroom. "Mom," our beautiful blonde said, "I'm praying that God will help me not to scream like I did last time!"

I was so grateful. With Karine's own words and God's continual presence, I knew we would all make it through.

And we did. The surgery was successful, and Karine was eager to follow the nurse's suggestion that she could help herself to as much ice cream as she wanted. We had just sailed through another milestone.

From the Inside Out

Chapter Nineteen

I treasured our family lifestyle. Rick and I owned a private counseling practice, the girls were thriving, and we were living in a season of blessing. When Melinda and Karine reached school age, we decided to educate them at home, something that fit hand-in-glove with our philosophy of life. We could give the girls individual attention, take family vacations during the year, and instruct them in faith. We were experiencing the excitement of raising a family, and we loved it.

The little church we attended was pastored by Rick's Dad, and we were actively involved. I taught Sunday School and eventually developed a program for children. It wasn't long before I was asked to hold the position of Director of Women's Ministry, and I gladly accepted, thrilled to have the opportunity to work more closely with women. Although our family was close, I was feeling the distinct absence of female friendships. Sometimes, between writing curriculum on my typewriter and returning calls on the phone, I would ask myself, *Why do I feel so alone?*

137

Being the planner I was, I felt comfortable with goals, schedules, and time lines. We always had a flurry of activity going on at home, and I thrived on "organized chaos". Then we decided it was time to remodel our home, one room at a time. Since there was little extra in the budget, the project sounded a bit crazy, but in a good way. We were sacrificing time and energy now for a prosperous investment in the future. Besides, I told myself, I loved having a full plate.

But something was amiss. The familiar pattern of homemaking, parenting, educating, counseling, directing, and now re-modeling, seemed to be off-balance. No longer was I getting a "buzz" from completing one task before I went to another. In search of that certain something that would end my day on a high note, I had started pulling time from my own sleep, working on projects after the girls were in bed. What had once been a satisfying feeling of accomplishment at day's end now only whetted my appetite for more. Every available moment was filled, if only with reading stories to the girls or going over the budget with Rick. I barely had time to kiss them all good-night before my mind was off and running again with a mental to-do list for the next morning.

One day I caught myself staring out the window of my home office. Melinda and Karine were down for their naps, and I had a few rare moments of silence in the house. I took a deep breath; I had six weeks of a Bible study curriculum to sketch out and a slew of phone calls to make.

Yet something stopped me. For once, I was still and quiet. I wasn't craving the next thing to do, the next "hit" of activity. I continued to stare out the window, watching the autumn breeze play through the leaves of the amber trees across the street. When was the last time I had simply enjoyed the breeze blowing through my hair? Stopped to drink a glass of ice tea in the fragrance of the luscious red roses in our front yard? Took in the breathtaking contrast of stunning white cumulus clouds against our cerulean high-desert skies? Within moments I recognized a still small voice speaking to me.

You are covering the pain of loneliness with work.

I blinked in disbelief. Did I hear right? Covering my pain of loneliness with work? How could that be? With my childhood on the farm, I had been surrounded with parents, grandparents, and siblings who worked constantly. Work was *good*; a necessary part of life. Work was abundant; vacations were few. Rest was limited to Sunday afternoons; time away from the farm meant visiting family.

But my counseling knowledge and experience confirmed the words I had heard in my spirit: I was lonely. And I was lonely because I was addicted to work. And I was addicted to work because I was

Linda A. Olson

lonely. A vicious cycle had seeped into my life, and I hadn't even noticed. I truly wanted to get to know women but had unconsciously filled my days with so much activity that I simply had no time to develop friendships. I was dumbfounded and slightly ashamed that I, a counselor and director, had allowed such an insidious, society-approved addiction to entangle my life. Dropping my head in silent agreement of using outward activity to cover inward pain, I asked God to help me deal with pain appropriately and to re-prioritize my life.

Then, in the midst of my new-found discovery and sincere attempt to alter my course, we changed churches. I was once again in a new environment where I knew no one. And loneliness was still begging to be my unseen companion. But this time I was determined to make friends. As the weeks passed and we became acquainted with more people, I wondered why, even when I initiated conversation with women, the relationships seldom went beyond small talk. I wasn't invited over for lunch, wasn't included in casual shopping trips, or wasn't even offered a cup of hot tea or coffee. No one called if I missed a service, if one of the girls had a fever or a runny nose, if life was falling apart for me in some way.

And then, after remembering the value of being still, I stopped my inward complaining and words again rose from the quiet of my spirit.

140

His Ways Are Higher

You cannot give what you do not have.

Another revelation. I considered the words for a few moments, letting the meaning of the phrase sink in. I knew I yearned for relationships; actually craved them. I wanted deep friendships with other women where we could explore faith and family, fears and fun. And, being who I was and with my experience, I thought I knew all there was to know about making friends.

But I was wrong.

Like fog disappearing from a clouded window, the truth became clear. I had judged these women—the very women in front of me whom I didn't know—to be shallow and unfriendly. With my leadership ability, I held their lack of initiative against them, and seeds of resentment had started to germinate.

But now I recognized those seeds, and I knew what to do with them. I was learning more about forgiveness. Now that I had forgiven myself, I realized I must ask God to forgive *me* for judging the hearts of these women. Then I would ask Him to help me forgive *them.* Without them even knowing, they had wounded me by their unwillingness to welcome me into their circle.

The need for forgiveness was becoming familiar and, instead of resisting the invitation to let go of blame, I began to embrace the freedom I knew existed beyond it. I also realized that a sincere love for new friends must first be grounded in a more intimate friendship between the Savior and myself.

I dropped to my knees and began my prayer, *"Oh, Lord, forgive me..."*

"Who, Me?"

Chapter Twenty

"Way to go!" I yelled with the other women. "Whoo-hoo! Hooray!" I applauded vigorously and then reached for my glass. The cool condensation from the ice water would feel good against my hands, reddened and stinging from continual clapping. I turned to my friend, one of seven, seated at our round table. We could see the platform in front clearly, although we sat near the back of the large banquet room. "Wow! Isn't this wonderful?"

These women, along with the other two thousand men and women in the room, knew what hard work was about. Their dedication had provided income, inspiration, and incentive to countless others in order to attend this evening of awards and public recognition within our marketing organization.

My own team, built over eleven years, had become like family to me. After years of heart-satisfying ministry in different churches while also serving clients in the secular arena of counseling, a major shift had occurred in my life. Our daughters, in high school at the time, would be home only a few more years and I wanted to treasure those years by being more available. The door to women's ministry—at one time a place where I had solid direction toward a national position—eventually closed firmly. Then the health care system changed insurance requirements for many of our counseling clients and I found I was spending more time shuffling paperwork than helping suicidal teenagers. After much prayer, Rick and I decided I would let go of my counseling practice to stay home and to supplement our income with focusing on a side business that seemed to be growing.

And grow it did. The leadership skills I had learned in earlier years now came to the forefront as I gladly helped other women attain unimagined growth in self-confidence, financial success, and personal satisfaction with our product.

And now here we were at the National Convention, applauding for women who were receiving top awards in sales, recruiting, and leadership development. I absent-mindedly twirled my wedding ring, wondering whose name would be called next.

It had been a tough go. Within several years of building my team, key members had approached the corporate office to separate themselves from my leadership. I was devastated. These women—the ones I had encouraged, supported, and befriended—now seemed to have become my enemies.

The feeling of betrayal once again began stalking my heart. .

*****

Forgiveness, I was learning, is not a one-time deal. Discovering that people are not who they seem often rocks our emotional boat, and the knee-jerk reaction is to pull away, withdraw. Our childhood response kicks in and we want to hurt back when we've been hurt.

Jesus said we are to forgive seventy times seven. I used to think that was a horrifically large list of offenses. But now I realize that four hundred and ninety may represent the unimaginable number of times a single offense may come to mind, and I must forgive again. Only the washing of continual forgiveness will fade the memory of hurt and betrayal, allowing for mercy and kindness to fuel any future relationship. These were hard lessons—difficult to learn, more difficult to practice.

But practice them I did, and I was becoming more quickly aware when seeds of bitterness were sown. One thing was in my power, however, and that was the decision whether or not to let those seeds land in fertile ground where they would sprout.

I decided to act quickly.

I caught that handful of seeds in mid-air, not waiting for them even to hit the ground of my heart. In a sudden, immediate decision borne out of years of earnest prayer with God about my own shortcomings and selfish desires, I immediately apologized for my part in the matter, asking forgiveness of those involved. Then I offered possible solutions to resolve the situation.

Naively I had thought that kindness begets kindness and, to be sure, that is true to some extent. But, in this situation, my apology was rejected outright and the next five years were peppered with phone calls from the attorney at our corporate office in an effort to find justifiable cause for the accusations from my own team.

But they were also five years filled with grace and peace as I prayed about the matter and talked with those in my life whose counsel I valued. I was asked if I not only had forgiven those who had accused me but had gone a step farther and asked God to bless them.

Eventually, through journaling and searching my own heart for any hidden motives, I did just that.

And then I was quiet.

My focus shifted from the legal battle with those who opposed me to the developing leadership in the remaining members of my team. My battle was trusted to the Lord, and I decided to set my mind on "whatsoever things are true, whatsoever things are honest, whatsoever things are just, whatsoever things are lovely, whatsoever things are of good report", according to Philippians 4:8. I kept my mouth shut, refusing to speak about the matter to anyone except Rick and the attorney, not wanting to approach even a hint of gossip.

*****

"And now, for our first place winner…" The emcee was looking at the paper in her hand and intentionally drawing out the announcement. The crowd roared. She held up her hand for quiet. "To the consultant and director who earned the most sales in this past year, whose team outranked all others in leadership development, and who most certainly deserves this recognition, we give this award to…" The emcee scanned the crowd. "…Linda Olson!"

I felt faint. Surely I had not heard correctly. I had not even tracked my numbers with exactness. Who me?

"Linda Olson, where are you?" The emcee was still looking for me "Come up here...you're Number One and we want to congratulate you!" Others in the room were turning in their seats to see who would stand.

My friends—my team—were pounding me on the back and cheering. "Linda, it's YOU! She means YOU! You did it! You're Number One!" In an instant, my mind flashed back to all that had happened, and all the grace and faithfulness the Lord had poured out on me. Only then did I gather myself together and run down the long aisle. It had been a long five years.

"I'm coming!" I called to the emcee.

Memory, Rest in Peace

Chapter Twenty One

"Vera, I am so glad to be here—what a wonderful day it's been! What a wonderful cook you are, and I'm so proud to be your sister." I raised my glass of sparkling cider to toast the host, second to the youngest of the Bergen clan.

"To Vera" The others around the family table echoed my sentiments as they raised their glasses to our hostess.

Seventeen of us had gathered together to celebrate an early Canadian Thanksgiving with delicious food, spell-binding storytelling, and side-splitting laughter. We had not been together in years and now here we were, well into the fourth, fifth, and sixth decades of our lives, enjoying the rich fellowship and satisfying companionability unique to family.

After everyone had taken a drink and the general murmurs had quieted a bit, I spoke again, addressing the other members of my family. "I want to thank you all for making this a special holiday for me. Thank you for driving three hundred miles to hear me speak. Being the keynote speaker at my alma mater was such a privilege, but an even greater privilege was looking into the crowd and knowing many of you were there. Thank you for your love and support. And, Dad," I turned to my aging father, once a man far distant from me emotionally, but who now—especially since Mom's death a few years ago—had become my greatest fan, "your being there, especially, meant the world to me. I am so grateful for you..." My eyes misted and I struggled to control my voice. I turned my gaze from his tear-filled eyes to look at each sibling at the table. "...and for you, and for you, and for you, and for you..." Their smiles eased the solemn moment into quiet nods of agreement.

My cup overflowed with gratitude. Our family had toured the campus after the harvest-time event the night before, talking about fun and old times, making the evening a pleasant stroll through memory lane as well as a time to talk about the current health of our families. All was well with each one of us, and we were basking in the peace of God's faithfulness.

Later, alone in my private guestroom, I reached for my laptop to journal my thoughts. Writing had always been an effective means of expressing my ponderings—my struggles and prayers as well as my gratitude. Somehow the feelings of my heart flowed more easily through my fingers than through my lips in spoken word. I wish I had actually spoken the words in a toast to my sister and acknowledged the family publicly for coming. Yes, I thanked each one individually but it never seemed enough. My heart was overwhelmed as my Dad sat with me at the table before I gave the keynote address. He had not even attended my graduation and now he was here, fully supportive of what I was doing and who I had become. He had no idea how God used his presence to heal my broken heart that day. Somehow, I felt intimidated when it came to speaking publicly in front of my family, but I truly wanted them to know how grateful I was. Silently, I prayed a little prayer asking God for forgiveness for not trusting Him for the courage to give public recognition to my family. They all deserved it.

Besides, by documenting my circumstances and my heart-responses to them, I had tangible tracking of God's movement in my life. As I opened the laptop, I glanced at the date. *September 26, 2010.*

Oh, wow.

Today marked the forty-fourth anniversary of little Billy's death.

*****

How appropriate that our family would gather together on this particular day. Indeed, where I had expected remnants of sorrow during my stay, I had experienced only welcome calm, as if our family was complete. I felt Billy's presence strong among us, and I knew that Mom was healed both physically and emotionally, her perpetual heartache having been finally eased by seeing Billy—and her Savior—face to face. From heaven, she too joined our family in sweet fellowship.

I began to type. "Lord, I am so grateful...."

*****

Tomorrow Vera and I would go for a long morning walk, something that was to become a brief routine during my week-long stay. Nothing compared to traversing the pathways on Canadian ground with one with whom I had shared a home. The slightly cool Canadian air felt so refreshing. I shivered unconsciously, mildly surprised that I had forgotten about autumn's annual drop in temperature.

In the comfortable silences during our conversation, I could hear our footsteps crunch the fallen leaves of the maple trees lining the street. My mind seemed to roll in reverse as I considered our sister-history together. Soon I pictured us as children, working side-by-side doing the chores after school.

And then I thought of Billy. Vera was eight years old—six years my junior—when Billy died. Consumed with my own grief over the years, I had never considered how the accident had affected my siblings. Carefully, so as to phrase my question without unnecessary intrusion into her own journey, I asked Vera about that day. I couldn't get my words out before the tears began to flow.

"Vera, I want you to know again that I am so sorry about what happened with Billy. You were so young, and I was so caught up in my own pain that I never asked about yours. May I ask you what you remember about that time?"

Vera, bless her heart, turned to me and smiled as she buttoned the top button of her lightweight cardigan. "Oh, Linda, are you still hurting over all of this? It's been way too long!" Vera pulled a tissue from her cardigan pocket and blew her nose. She put her arm around me as we walked. The breeze swirled maple leaves in the air. "No", I said, "this time I want to hear about you. I know that you carried a load way beyond what anyone should at your age". Vera looked up at the maples near the house and slowed her pace while she mentally replayed the horrific years following the accident. Slowly, choosing her words carefully at first, she began to open her heart to me. I listened without comment and before we knew it we were at the back door of the house. Pausing in our conversation, we brushed fallen leaves from our hair, removed our shoes and headed into the kitchen to put the teakettle on.

Soon our hands were warming around mugs of hot tea and Vera shared with me some of her pain. "The hardest part was after Irma was born. Mom and Dad were not getting along. Everyone was just trying to cope. A few years later you left for college, Vi was working in Winnipeg and I felt like I was left to raise Irma. I used to get such horrible headaches from all the stress and I finally quit school because it was too much". .

I rose to give Vera a big hug and said, "I'm so sorry you had to go through all this. No one your age should have ever had to carry the responsibility of a parent." We hugged and cried together as the hurt of the past disssolved with the tears. We talked more then, Vera and I. My heart broke to learn that she too had gone through years of heartache unspeakable, her own valley of grief and sorrow. She had been closer to Billy than I had thought. We cried more that day, peppering our conversation with nods of remembrance, of purposefully searching our minds to talk about the little boy who had stolen our hearts so many years ago. Somehow, sharing these intimate moments with each other brought a closer bond than we had ever known.

By the end of the week our baby sister Irma— younger than me by sixteen years—took us on a tour of the camp property near Winkler. Irma, born two years after Billy's death, had no memory of the accident, of course. Yet she grew up into a family stricken by profound loss, and she always wondered why silence and a sense of sadness filled our home so much. As she matured, Vera shared more details of the accident with her, and in her own quiet way, she filled a big gap, eager to listen to stories about Billy but unaffected emotionally by them. Her tender heart became a strength for the family. Remembering those years, I knew Irma—with her position as the youngest child in the family and with her caring heart—had provided a lasting place of refuge in our lives after Billy moved to heaven. Perhaps her very existence was the blessing we needed after Billy's home-going.

As I returned to California, I also called Karen, my three-and-a-half-year-old cousin who had also been crushed by the tractor I was driving. Her injuries from the accident were limited to a ruptured kidney, but her memories of that time centered mainly on her experience in the hospital. She remembered how kind the nurses had been, how compassionate and gentle they were when they changed her bandages, how they always made her laugh when her care necessitated uncomfortable and even painful washing of her wounds. Her three-day hospital stay—and the nurses' extraordinary kindness— influenced the direction of her life, planting seeds of a future career to help others. Today Karen is a medical family practitioner, a doctor serving those in the Manitoba community.

Violet, my eldest sibling, was next. Our conversation brought to her mind the terrific responsibility she felt after the tragedy happened. She, at seventeen years old, bridged the young children with the adults in the family, yet she often felt caught in the middle, wanting to help ease the bewilderment of the young ones while desperately attempting to carry on daily life like the adults. Mom, in the grief-filled days following Billy's death, struggled to function with the most rudimentary tasks like getting simple meals on the table, overseeing baths and bedtimes. Dad dealt with his grief alone in the fields. When he and Len did approach the house, they stomped their feet on the front porch to clean their shoes of the hay and mud before washing up for a meal. In the evenings, they silently nodded goodnight and headed to bed. So Violet felt she had to step in to fill the gaps. She knew the dirty clothes had to be washed, supper needed to be made and the chores had to get done, but what really broke her heart was witnessing the playing-out of the family's grief. She said she so badly wanted to take all of us kids and escape somewhere so we were not submitted to Mom and Dad yelling at each other, but there was no place to go and she had no money. Violet herself ached tremendously— but she, too, often felt helpless. Nothing could fill the hole that little Billy left in our home.

*****

His Ways Are Higher

One by one my siblings expressed to me their lack of condemnation for my actions on that day forty-four years ago. "I hope you know that we have never held this against you," Vera had told me. And I knew that to be true—not a one had exhibited anything but love to me since Billy's death. Still, hearing their words soothed my soul, and I felt forgiveness flow into the cracks of my heart.

Back home in California, I called my brother Len on the telephone. Len had been twelve years old that day so long ago. He remembered Billy's favorite song Kumbaya. The title, which means *Come by here, Lord* so accurately reflected Billy's heart for God, Len told me. The death of his little brother had completely changed the future of daily life for Len: a farm is run by the boys and men in the family and Len, now the only living son, had grown up with the full brunt of the farm chores, working alongside Dad and then, eventually, inheriting total responsibility for the running of the family homestead. Many times, he told me, that was more of a burden than a privilege. Len also shared with me something that struck a cord within me.

"Did you know that Billy begged to go on the tractor with me that day?" he said. Len and Dad had been headed out to work a field about half a mile away. "I was only twelve years old and I knew Mom and Dad wouldn't permit it." And so Billy was so upset because he could not go with his older "bruvver". We talked a few more minutes, and I thanked him for sharing so openly with me about the incident all these many years later.

As I hung up the phone I stepped into the kitchen, just as Rick came home from work. Tears flowed as I shared with him my conversation with Len. We moved to the family room where I sunk into the dark blue comfy couch with Rick listening through my sobs. I hadn't known about Billy's wanting to go on the tractor with Len. But that brought up a question that had been hidden in my heart a long time. *Why was I the one driving the tractor that day? Why was I the one sitting on that huge piece of machinery that failed to stop and that plowed into my little brother, crushing him to death?*

And then something happened.

A story I had heard a few years before sprang to mind. A woman had been horrendously abused as a child, resulting in adult difficulties so profound she had been told she would need to use psychiatric medication the rest of her life. But a new doctor showed her a picture of a brain, explaining how different parts of the brain relate to different things. He had asked the woman, "Has anyone ever told you why your dad chose to abuse you as opposed to your brother and sister?"

She had shaken her head, puzzled. "Well, no."

His Ways Are Higher

The doctor explained. "It is because your dad knew you would always love him. Your brother and sister would most likely get to a certain age and completely sever any relationship with your father. But you, he knew, would always be there for him—even though he caused you so much pain."

Now, clear as a bell, I heard the still small voice speak to my heart.

"*I chose you*"

You chose me? How could this be? You mean this was part of Your plan all along, God? I sat up straighter.

"*I chose you because of your strength*".

My strength? I certainly didn't feel strong when I couldn't stop the brakes of the tractor. Then I heard the voice again,

"*I chose you because of your strength, Linda, because I knew your faith was stronger than your emotional pain. I knew that you would always love me.*"

As I began to reflect on my journey, I could easily verify that I had not wandered from God. As difficult as things were I stayed close to Him. It was the only way I knew I would make it. I was the one on the tractor that day because I was the one who would always love Jesus no matter what.

And then the Holy Spirit spoke again. "*I knew that someday you would rise above your pain and share your story for My glory.*"

Attempting to catch my breath, I questioned myself. *Did this really just happen or did I just make this up*?

NO! I knew I hadn't made this up. It was so clear. It had to have been an unexpected visit from the Holy Spirit. I had never experienced this before so I remained quiet, trying to absorb what had just happened and let it soak in.

God had just answered my life-long question, the one I didn't think would be answered this side of heaven.

No matter how much I hurt, no matter how much I didn't understand, somehow I always knew the accident was just that: an accident. I never once blamed God for Billy's death; I only questioned endlessly the events that surrounded it. Now I knew beyond a shadow of a doubt that God allowed me to be on the tractor, not because of emotional weakness, but because I possessed emotional strength. God knew that my love for Him would ultimately prove to be greater than my emotional pain. God had answered my deepest innermost question. Of course, I couldn't help but wonder why

His Ways Are Higher

He waited forty-four years to answer... and then I knew.

My ways are higher, He reminded me.

Amen to that! I answered in my spirit.

"It's Alright, Nina"

Chapter Twenty Two

I held the book and stared into space. *Heaven is for Real* is the story of a little boy who had a near-death experience in a surgical ward. Colton often surprised his parents in the months following emergency surgery after a burst appendix by talking about Jesus and heaven and people he had seen there.

*****

One person Colton had met in Heaven was his older sister who had died in a miscarriage, a sibling his parent had never mentioned. Colton spoke of how the little girl ran up to him and "wouldn't stop hugging me".

*****

My eyes misted as I closed the book. A picture of Billy immediately came to mind. How I wish I could hug my baby brother like Colton's sister had hugged him.

In the years since the accident, I had done all I knew to clear my mind from distorted and destructive thinking. I had approached the Lord with a sincere desire akin to the psalmist's: *"Search me, O God, and know my heart: try me, and know my thoughts: And see if there be any wicked way in me"* (Psalm 139:23, 24). And time after time, I had worked through everything that came up. Now I was surprised to discover that, tucked deep down in a corner of my heart, something else disturbed me.

My Canadian upbringing had instilled in me a tremendous sense of hard-work-brings-tangible-rewards work ethic. Although I knew that my salvation in Christ rested in His atoning death on the cross and not on anything I could do, the working out of that principle had been just that: working. Now, after many years of study and walking with the Lord, my "works" arsenal included powerful weapons of spiritual warfare: Bible study, communion with Christ Himself, prayer, and solid knowledge of who I was in Christ. Yet sometimes I could feel the enemy advance in my life.

It seemed that every autumn as the weather turned cool and the leaves began to fall, I would have this horrible ache in the pit of my stomach. The ache was constant, always appearing about a month before the anniversary of the accident and lasting until right around the anniversary date. I prayed and prayed that God would take it away, reminding myself that the devil's shouts of condemning accusations were only empty threats. I knew his accusations were not true, and I knew that God's Word says, "...you will know the truth, and the truth will set you free" (John 8:32), so I didn't accept the accusations.

I would struggle to recall my training, actively put on my spiritual armor listed in Ephesians 6, and get ready to wield my spiritual weapons. Then I would declare the truth to the enemy: "*I am redeemed, restored, and reconciled with God. He created me and has purchased me with the blood of His own Son Jesus Christ. I am forgiven, washed clean, and made a new creation. The Lord has knit me together in my mother's womb and knows all my days. He loves me and has great purpose for me...*"

And so the battle went. The enemy would stalk me, his tirades escalating from whispers to ear-splitting decibel levels in my spirit, and I would resist. I knew that if I resisted the devil with truth, he would be forced to flee (James 4:7). Yet the frequent battles exhausted me. Desperate, I asked God to reveal the weak area in me that allowed the devil to still have a stronghold. Immediately I remembered hearing of an annual prayer conference coming up that I had attended before. Since these women were particularly gifted in hearing and discerning the Holy Spirit, I decided this was my next step.

Linda A. Olson

At the conference I discovered, surprisingly, that the devil had set me up long before the accident with condemning spirits of fear, abandonment, torment and intimidation. I had always targeted the accident as the cause of the battle since I was still being tormented. Several ladies prayed for me, and I was set free and given the words, "healing, deliverance and restoration" on which to mediatate. I was also told that God was taking me through a type of refiner's fire because He had so much in store for me. My heart overflowed with thanksgiving, and I had a deep desire to simply be faithful to Him and obedient, giving Him my very best. The evil spirits had been identified and if they tried coming at me again, I knew exactly how to resist them and cast them off. I was set free.

A year after I spoke to my siblings about the accident, God was continuing to do a deep work in me, and my heart was vulnerable. One morning, as Rick and I walked the familiar two-mile route around our neighborhood, I found myself stopping several times to catch my breath.

"What is wrong with me?" I told Rick with frustration. *" I thought I was in better physical shape than this. Next time, I go to the chiropractor's I'm going to talk to him about this."*

166

His Ways Are Higher

As I met with the chiropractor-now-become-friend, having accompanied me on my journey through my emotional as well as physical pain, he checked my heart and said, "*There is nothing wrong with your heart physically, Linda, but you are still dealing with a broken heart regarding the accident with your little brother.*"

Suddenly I wanted to scream. Instead I carefully controlled my voice. "*When is this ever going to be over?*"

*****

Dr. Emard has asked if I had read, *Heaven is for Real*. When I told him I hadn't, he basically prescribed it. He said, "*I would like you to read it this weekend. It will be healing for you.*" So I agreed.

And now here I was, pondering how little Colton could possibly know that he had an older sister in heaven.

The following week I returned to the chiropractor and he asked if I had read the book. I said, "*Yes, and you are right; it was very healing.*"

And then he said something astonishing. "*God showed me that when you have a conversation with your little brother, you will be completely healed.*"

I was shocked and speechless. Dr. Emard had worked with our family for many years and I trusted his insights, so I received what he said, although with some inward questions. As I walked out of his office, I prayed. *Okay, God, how do You want me to do this? Do I just start talking as if Billy was here?* I hadn't seen any supernatural visions of Billy, and I wasn't sure how to begin an interview with the little towhead who had joined the cloud of witnesses nearly forty-five years before. I *had* spoken with each family member about the accident, and our conversations had brought back sweet memories of Billy. But recalling memories was not the same as having a live encounter. The rest of the evening, I pondered Dr. Emard's words and consciously alerted my spiritual ears to listen for God's direction.

*****

The following day, my husband and I packed our bags and went on a brief vacation to the beach, my favorite place to unwind. But before I could fully relax I wanted to journal the many things God was revealing to me. Sitting on the couch, I opened my

laptop and began. Soon I couldn't punch the keys on my computer fast enough, and the tears were rolling down my cheeks. The Holy Spirit had come upon me and I was in conversation with Billy.

*****

His Ways Are Higher

"*Billy! Oh, Billy...*" I was down on one knee, embracing my precious baby brother. Joy unspeakable had entered my soul.

His little-boy arms squeezed tight around my neck as he whispered in my ear, "*I am so happy to see you!*"

I melted at his sweet baby lisp. My eyes were wet, my voice making its way around the lump in my throat. I held him close, feeling his heartbeat. "*Me, too, Billy. I have missed you so much.*" Oh, how I wanted to stay like that forever, feeling his arms around me, his baby-child breath on my cheek. He was dressed in his favorite overalls, a blue plaid shirt matching his baby blue eyes.

Billy drew back and touched my face with his chubby fingers. "*I know, Nina...*"

I melted again. Nina was his nickname for me.

He brushed back a wisp of my hair. "*Jesus told me how hard you prayed that I wouldn't die, but He said He needed me in Heaven. I asked Him, 'Why can't Nina and I be together?' And He said that I had finished my job already but He had more for you to do.*"

I smiled at his language. We had always loved to talk together. For a little boy, he had an uncanny ability to communicate.

He spoke again. "*I remember His words, Nina*! He said, '*When Nina completes her work on earth, then we can all be together forever and ever and ever.*'"

Billy's big blue eyes gazed into mine. I couldn't seem to get enough of just looking at him, drinking in his boyish splendor. "*Nina, I'm having so much fun! There are so many kids to play with, and Jesus loves us so much. I can hardly wait until you come.*"

I cradled his face with my hands. "*Billy, I will do whatever Jesus asks me to do, and then I'll come as quickly as I can.*" Time seemed to stand still, as if the past, present, and future had all come together at once. I sensed that my lifetime on earth would go by as quickly as the snap of my fingers.

We embraced again. I wanted to memorize the feel of his arms circling my neck, the smell of his boyish scent, the voice that used to sing Kum-by-yah over and over again.

He squeezed me hard. "*Okay, Nina. You'll love heaven, too. It's so beautiful here. And, Nina...*" He pulled back, looked at me directly and said, "*There is one more thing.*"

"*What's that*?" I said, not wanting to miss one word. With his hand, he wiped away the tears that had brimmed over on my face. "*I don't want you to be sad anymore. I am so happy here. I couldn't be happier. I'm having so much fun. Please don't be sad.*" And then his little voice perked up, "*And you know what?*"

"*What?*" I said, eager to smile again.

He grinned. "*There are no tears in heaven!*" And we laughed together.

One more hug.

I knew now I could let him go. Although I had not spoken my apology aloud, it was as if our hearts had filled in the words. Somehow I knew Billy did not hold anything against me; he had forgiven me for the accident from the moment he had been hurt. All apprehension that I had caused him pain and sorrow simply evaporated, and I knew all was well between us.

"*Bye, Billy. I love you!*" I sensed our visit was coming to an end.

"*'Bye, Nina! I love you too!*" He smiled one more time and turned away. As he ran off, I stood and watched, and the picture in my mind began to fade. Billy turned, blew me a kiss, and the picture faded completely.

*****

Still frantically pushing the keys on my laptop, I stopped for a moment and glanced at the clock. It was two minutes after midnight on September 26th

— the 45th anniversary of Billy's accident. Today was the first day in forty-five years that I could celebrate the day instead of grieve.

My glimpse of Billy in heaven had given me a completely new perspective. Billy could not be happier. And now condemning myself seemed to serve no purpose at all; guilt had been completely removed.

I saw that God had a much bigger plan than just the plan for my life, or even for Billy's life. We were both simply part of a larger plan and I knew that, from this day forward, the enemy would have no place in my life to form a stronghold about Billy's death. I had received freedom—pure, abundant, permanent freedom—and I would live the rest of my days in gratefulness. Indeed, Satan had meant to destroy not only Billy's life that fateful September afternoon, but mine as well.

But he had NOT succeeded. What he had meant for evil, God had turned into good. It was *good* for Billy to be with Jesus. It was *good* for me to remain on earth. It was *good* for me to walk in freedom, to be healed of the heartache I had carried with me for forty-five years. It was *good* for me to know I would see Billy one day. It was *good* that God was in all, over all, through all. My soul sang silent hallelujahs.

His Ways Are Higher

As my husband and I drove alongside the ocean, catching glimpses of the seagulls playing in the sand, the waves rolling in to celebrate with us, I noticed the truck in front of us had a sticker on the back window with a cross and a little boy with the name "Billy". God had one more time confirmed to me that He was caring for Billy.

And now I knew why Mom, after Billy died and on those rare occasions when I would see peace on her face, would quietly sing her favorite song *Heaven Came Down and Glory Filled My Soul.* Sometimes when we yearn for those who have gone before, when grief is unspeakable and when the distance between us and those we love seems too far, too high, too hidden, it is then that God Himself somehow bridges the gap, and brings heaven to earth for awhile.

Afterward

Looking back over my life, I see a thread that began before I was born. That thread—pulled tight through the fabric of my days on the farm, in and out through the garments of childhood and adolescence, and knotted at the time of Billy's accident—connected remnant pieces of cloth of my existence. The thread wove a seam pairing my college experiences with ministry opportunities, and then it secured the delicate and beautiful buttons of my husband and our two daughters. I see the thread today as it holds together the patchwork quilt of my days—so different from what I originally had in mind but wonderful in its history and declaration of life.

The thread is forgiveness, held in the needle of the Holy Spirit and sewn with the love of Christ Jesus Himself. He took what I saw as random experiences, painful with grief and loss, and sewed them with this amazing thread, forgiving me and teaching me to forgive.

For my part, I see that I had a choice: would I allow the patches to be joined together by love Himself? Would I allow Him free movement in my life? Would I allow Him to take the hard experience with Billy and sew it together with my family? Would I allow His mercy to go in and out of the hurts and betrayals, the confusions and the seeds of bitterness? Surely He had the power to make all things new, but I also realized something was required of me. Would I allow Him to carry His love and forgiveness in and out, in and out of broken relationships, of my own pain and condemnation? Did I have the strength and courage to allow Him to create what He wanted in my life?

I did.

The decision to receive Christ into my life was the foundation for my survival on that late September afternoon when Billy died. My recovery depended on the truth of His word, His faithfulness to me, and His hope for my future.

I would like you to know Him too.

What does that mean? Simply, the decision to welcome Christ is acknowledged through prayer. God loves us; He really does. He created us out of love to be who we are, and He rejoices in our uniqueness. He desires our company, and invites us into relationship with Him. Down through the ages, He has let mankind know of His love for us, first by sending people who knew Him to spread the word, and then by sending His son Jesus to earth to live life just like we do, with all its hardness and perplexities and despair. He was the perfect representation of His

His Ways Are Higher

Father, yet we didn't believe Him when He came. Our own wrongdoing—and wrong thinking—caused us collectively as a people to hurt Him, torture Him, and eventually kill Him, all because He said He was God. And yet, from God's point of view, Jesus was taking the place that had awaited *us*; we were the ones who were really doomed to death because of our own rejection of Him.

But death did not hold Him. Jesus rose from the dead and He lives today. Through Him our sin is obliterated and we have freedom from its stranglehold. We live forever with Him, starting from the moment we ask His forgiveness. God didn't relish seeing Jesus go through suffering, and He doesn't relish it when we go through it. But He did know that, ultimately, Christ would suffer on our behalf. To that end, He offers us salvation—He saves us from ourselves, from our sin, and from eternal separation from God.

He doesn't push this salvation—He simply offers it. Picture Him like a bridegroom saying, "*Do you receive Me*?" He stands with hopeful expectancy, waiting for the sincere answer from His bride, "*I do*".

God hears the words of sincere hearts, and His Son is a most trustworthy gentleman. Christ will do as He promised and, by the Holy Spirit at your invitation, will enter your heart to reside there forever, to be your closest friend, your truest brother, your most faithful guide.

If you would like to personally know this Bridegroom who constantly declares His love for you, you might express your heart to Him with words like these:

"God, I come to you acknowledging that I have done wrong, and that my life is empty without you. I'm sorry; please forgive me. I understand that Jesus is your Son and that you sent Him to earth to show me who you really are, and I understand that His sacrificial death has paved the way for me to approach you. I would like to start again. Jesus, I thank you for your love for me and do now receive it. Please come into my life. With all my heart, I thank you."

*****

If you have invited Christ into your life, I encourage you to enjoy His fellowship!

Ask Him to bring other believers across your path, and begin reading the Bible to know more about Him.

The book of John (in the Bible) is a good place to start. The Holy Spirit will reveal Truth Himself and will direct you in your everyday life and decisions.

I would love to have the opportunity to welcome you personally into the family of God.

*Email me at **linda@madeforsomethingmore** and tell me about your experience.*

If you would like more information about speaking, speaker training, or telling your story, please check out...

"What's Your Story?" *blog or visit me at* ***www.madeforsomethingmore.com*** ***www.wealththroughstories.com***

I look forward to meeting you.

Asking God to bless you abundantly,

Linda

About the Author

Linda's new book *His Ways Are Higher, One Woman's Journey to Self-Forgiveness Against Unbeatable Odds* is her 45-year journey to complete victory. Within her big story are many smaller stories, the valuable lessons that have become treasures to her.

Packaging the lessons she learned Linda sets out to help ordinary people tell their extra-ordinary story. She works with speakers, business owners and entrepreneurs who are committed to learning the skill of great storytelling.

Linda Olson is an International speaker, author, coach and CEO of Wealth Through Story. One of her greatest strengths is her ability to captivate audiences of every age with her storytelling ability. Large audiences, small groups or a one-on-one contact find their hearts drawn in and are mesmerized by Linda's passion and inspiration as she unfolds valuable lessons through storytelling.

With more than 40 years of experience, Linda is an expert in helping speakers, business owners and entrepreneurs break through to fulfilling their dream.

Linda A. Olson

As a Marriage & Family therapist she focused on breakthroughs from the inside out. As a network marketer, she quickly soared to the top 3-4% in her company and remained there for 24 years bringing in over $2 Million annually with her team.

As a ministry leader, she became the entrepreneur of a woman's program at a church of over 5,000 attendees.

Linda loves finding ordinary people and helping them become a greater influence, impact more people and increase their bottom line through the art of great storytelling. It is the #1 way to connect with people and make a difference.

Linda's passions include traveling, photo journaling, spending time with her husband, family & adorable grandchildren. Although born and raised in Manitoba, Canada, Linda journeyed to California to pursue her Masters in Counseling in 1980. Two years later she met and married the man of her dreams. Rick and Linda make their home in Palmdale, California.

Isn't it time to get
that book out of
your head and
into the hands of the
people who need it?

www.ABookIsNeverABook.com

God gets the Glory
when you
TELL your story!
– Kathleen D. Mailer

CHRISTIANAUTHORSGETPAID.com

183

SPEAKER

LINDA A OLSON
CEO of Wealth Through Stories
Speaker/Trainer Program

Inspirational!

Experiential!

Transformational!

It's not what you
give them but
what they leave
with that makes
a difference.

www.LindaAOlson.com
www.WealthThroughStories.com

linda@madeforsomethingmore.com

Made in the USA
San Bernardino, CA
02 March 2017